Edexcel International GCSE Geography

Edexcel Certificate in Geography

Revision Guide

Rob Bircher

WAYS LEARNING

PEARSON

Published by Pearson Education Limited, Edinburgh Gate, Harlow, Essex, CM20 2JE.

www.pearsonglobalschools.com

Copies of official specifications for all Edexcel qualifications may be found on the Edexcel website: www.edexcel.com

Text © Pearson Education Limited 2013
Edited by Sue Thomas
Proofread by Katherine James
Original design by Richard Ponsford
Typeset by Phoenix Photosetting
Original illustrations © Pearson Education Limited 2013
Indexed by Indexing Specialists (UK) Ltd.

The right of Rob Bircher to be identified as author of this work has been asserted by him in accordance with the Copyright, Designs and Patents Act 1988.

First published 2013

17 16 15 14 13
IMP 10 9 8 7 6 5 4 3 2 1

British Library Cataloguing in Publication Data
A catalogue record for this book is available from the British Library

ISBN 978 1 446 90577 7

Acknowledgements
The author and publisher would like to thank the following individuals and organisations for permission to reproduce photographs in the book and ebook:

(Key: b-bottom; c-centre; l-left; r-right; t-top)

Alamy Images: 18t, 33c, Bill Brooks 58bl, Craig Buchanan 28tr, david pearson 72cl, Frans Lanting Studio 65t, Frederique Cifuentes Morgan 58tl, Hans Lippert 54tr, incamerastock 44b, Malcolm Park English coastline 13tr, Oleksiy Maksymenko 71c, Spaces Images 55c, travelib prime 13tl; **Fotolia.com:** tomalu 14b; **Getty Images:** Bloomberg via Getty Images 73b, Getty Images 79b, Globe Turner, LLC 76br; **Science Photo Library Ltd:** RIA NOVOSTI 62bl

Cover images: *Front:* **PhotoDisc**

All other images © Pearson Education

The publisher would also like to thank the following for their kind permission to reproduce their photographs in the ebook only:

Alamy Images: CuboImages srl (volcano), David Bagnall (River Severn), imagebroker (Opel), Janine Wiedel Photolibrary (Asylum seekers), Joe Bird (Site 2012 Olympics)

In some instances we have been unable to trace the owners of copyright material, and we would appreciate any information that would enable us to do so.

Every effort has been made to contact copyright holders of material reproduced in this book. Any omissions will be rectified in subsequent printings if notice is given to the publishers.

Websites
Pearson Education Limited is not responsible for the content of any external internet sites. It is essential for tutors to preview each website before using it in class so as to ensure that the URL is still accurate, relevant and appropriate. We suggest that tutors bookmark useful websites and consider enabling students to access them through the school/college intranet.

A note from the publisher
In order to ensure that this resource offers high-quality support for the associated Edexcel qualification, it has been through a review process by the awarding organisation to confirm that it fully covers the teaching and learning content of the specification or part of a specification at which it is aimed, and demonstrates an appropriate balance between the development of subject skills, knowledge and understanding, in addition to preparation for assessment.

While the publishers have made every attempt to ensure that advice on the qualification and its assessment is accurate, the official specification and associated assessment guidance materials are the only authoritative source of information and should always be referred to for definitive guidance.

Edexcel examiners have not contributed to any sections in this resource relevant to examination papers for which they have responsibility.

No material from an endorsed resource will be used verbatim in any assessment set by Edexcel.

Endorsement of a resource does not mean that the resource is required to achieve this Edexcel qualification, nor does it mean that it is the only suitable material available to support the qualification, and any resource lists produced by the awarding organisation shall include this and other appropriate resources.

Contents

Using the book

It's often difficult to know where to start with revision! This guide breaks the content of the course down, topic by topic, to help you revise effectively and learn what you need to know for your International GCSE Geography or Certificate in Geography exam.

Revision advice

Here you will find advice and tips on the best way to approach your revision. Every student is different so it's important to work out which method suits you best. You may want to try out a few to see which works for you.

Chapter summaries

The revision guide is structured around the chapters in the Student Book. Each of these chapter summaries contains the key learning points, with diagrams and photos to help you revise. Look out for Top tip and Key fact (green) boxes to help you prepare as effectively as possible for the exam. Use the worksheets and interactive quizzes in the e-book to help you revise each chapter.

Remember that there are many different case studies and examples in Geography and the ones you have studied in class are the ones you should revise – the examples in this book are not as detailed as those you will have learned in school.

Remember, too, that you do not need to revise every topic in this book. You will have studied **two** out of the three topics in Section A, **two** out of three in Section B and **one** out of three in Section D. Revise only what you need to!

Exam-style questions

At the end of each chapter there is a list of questions for you to try. They are in a similar style to the Edexcel International GCSE Geography/Edexcel Certificate in Geography exams so they will help you practise for your examination as well as test how well you have understood each topic.

Exam preparation

The final section of the book looks at preparing for your exams. It gives you detailed exam advice, including advice on examination language, how the exams are laid out, how to do well in them, common pitfalls and how to demonstrate your skills and knowledge as well as you possibly can. The glossary at the back of the book explains key words and all glossary terms have been made bold the first time they appear in the book.

Organising your revision

The key to revision success is being organised. Here are a few ideas on how to structure your revision:

- **Manage your time effectively:** Revising for hours at a time will not help you remember. It is important to take regular breaks. Most people find it difficult to concentrate for more than 20–30 minutes at a time. To break up your revision sessions, relax for 5 minutes at regular intervals. Take a longer break every hour and a half, perhaps by going for a walk or talking to someone. Some people can revise for longer periods at a time. If that suits you, then perhaps take a short break every 45 minutes. The night before the exam, make sure you get a good night's sleep. Don't try to read through everything again. If you have revised effectively, at most you will only need to have a quick look at your notes.

When you have finished the map, put it away and then repeat the process. Did you include the same things? Compare the two maps and then draw a third one to include all topics from both maps. There may be some you thought of the second time that weren't on the first map.

Using a standard approach

Case studies are the most difficult things to revise in Geography because there are so many of them. It is easy to get them confused with each other and they are full of detail that is hard to keep track of. Then when it comes to the exam, you have to make them fit the question – it's no good just writing down everything you can remember and hoping some of it is relevant.

A good way to revise case studies is to look at their essential key facts and learn those by writing them on cards.

Let's look at an example from topic 2, Coastal environments: a case study of a retreating coastline – causes, impacts and management. Your card might have headings like this:

Topic 2: Retreating coastline case study

Name and location:

Causes of retreat:

Impacts:
- economic
- social
- environmental

Management
- strategy 1
- strategy 2

Improving your memory

- **Sticky notes:** There are a lot of specialist terms in Geography, and quite a few initials to remember as well! To help you remember them, write words and definitions on sticky notes or small cards and leave them in places where you will see them every day, for example around your bedroom or on the bathroom mirror. The Key fact boxes in this book tell you what you really need to know.

- **Mnemonics:** To make a mnemonic, take the first letters of the words you need to remember and make up a phrase you can easily remember. For example, the global distribution of coral reefs is controlled by four factors:

  temperature → light → water depth → salinity

  If you take the first letters of each of these factors you could make the following mnemonic to help you remember them: **tiny little wiggling slugs** – though it would be better if it related more closely to the topic!

- **Read, cover, write, check:** Read through a short unit of work several times. Once you feel that you know it, cover it up and write down all the main points that you can remember. Check what you have written against the unit and add anything that you have forgotten in a different colour. This will remind you what to focus on when you revisit the topic.

- **Flow diagrams:** A flow chart or spider diagram can help you learn a sequence of things. Look at the diagram, then put it away and draw it again. Compare the two versions and mark what you didn't remember in a different colour so you can focus on it when you look at it again.

- **Record what you need to learn:** If you learn best by listening, rather than reading, then record what you want to learn on your mobile phone, mp3 player or computer and listen back to it. It can also make revision more fun!

- **Find a revision partner:** There are many ways in which you could revise with a friend. You could read aloud to each other or invent tests for each other.

Practice questions

Practice questions really help you to see if you have learned a topic well. They also help you understand what to expect in the exam and introduce you to the language used in an exam. There are practice questions at the end of each chapter of this revision guide as well as a Some tips for the exam section at the end of the book that gives you advice on how to answer questions well and an introduction to how your work will be assessed. Make sure you read this section before practising any questions.

Revision checklist

- **Start your revision as early as possible:** start at least two months before the exam. If you leave it too late you can feel rushed, and if you come across something you don't understand there is less time for you to get to grips with it.

- **Plan your time:** make sure you have enough time to revise everything you need to. You could make yourself a timetable and tick things off as you complete them.

- **Break up your revision:** splitting it into manageable chunks makes it a less scary prospect!

- **Vary the way you revise:** make lists, write summaries, draw spider diagrams or record your revision: this helps you learn in different ways and is more effective than just reading through your notes.

- **Check you understand your work:** if you don't understand something, go back to the Student Book or ask your teacher.

- **Revise your practical geographical enquiry skills** for Section A and Section B topics.

- **Practise answering exam questions:** this will help you familiarise yourself with examination language and understand what the examiner expects you to do.

Good luck!

Chapter 1: River environments

The hydrological cycle

The hydrological cycle is a closed system – there is a fixed amount of water on Earth that is constantly recycled.

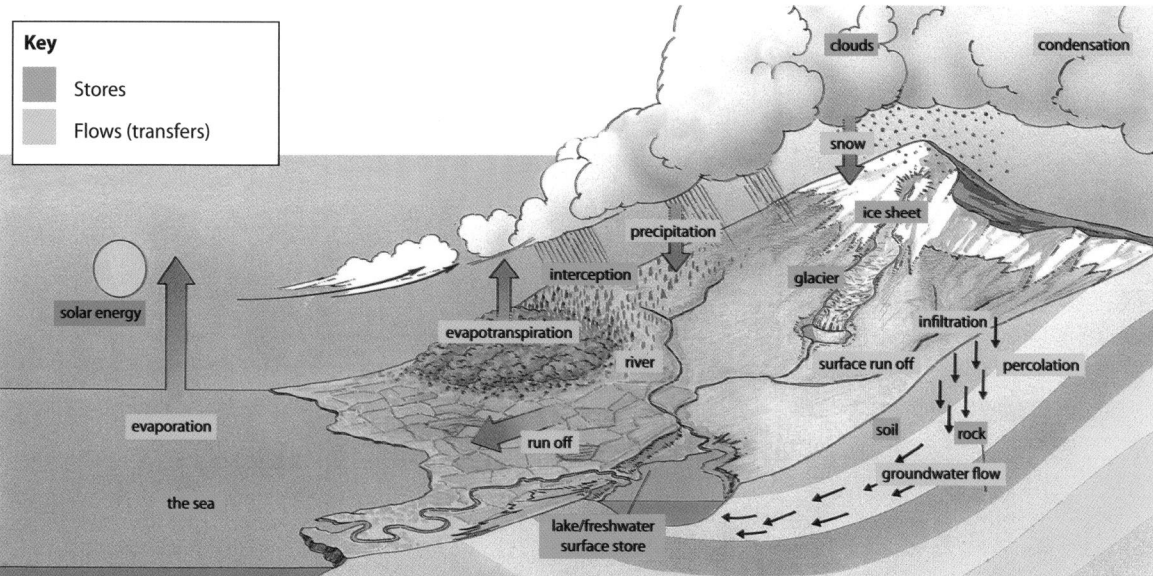

Figure 1.1 *The hydrological cycle: water is held in **stores** and moves between them in **transfers***

Stores

- The **atmosphere** – water is held as water vapour or droplets in clouds.

- The **land** – water is held in ice sheets, glaciers and snowfields; in lakes, rivers and reservoirs; in vegetation; and as groundwater in the soil or bedrock.

- The **sea**.

95 per cent of the Earth's water is stored in the sea.

Transfers

- **Evaporation** – important in transferring water from the sea to the atmosphere.

- **Transpiration** – the transfer of water vapour into the atmosphere by plants.

- **Precipitation** – water **condenses** in the atmosphere and then transfers from the atmosphere to the land or sea surface as rain, hail or snow.

- **Overland flow** – precipitation that runs off the ground surface into a stream, river or lake.

- **Infiltration/percolation** – the transfer of water through the soil into the groundwater store.

- **Throughflow** – water that doesn't enter groundwater but moves slowly through the soil until it reaches a stream or river.

- **Groundwater flow** – the underground transfer of water to rivers, lakes and the sea.

Drainage basins and their features

Each drainage basin has a unique combination of different features such as size, shape, rock types, relief and land use.

The **watershed** marks the dividing line between neighbouring drainage basins. Most precipitation happens in the upland areas near the watershed.

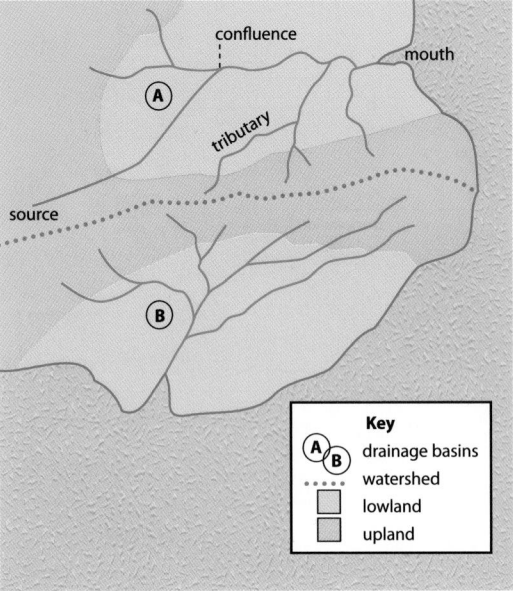

Figure 1.2 *Drainage basin features*

FIELDWORK INVESTIGATION

Channel networks can be mapped and their lengths and densities measured and compared.

The **channel network** is the system of surface and underground channels that collect and transport the precipitation that falls on the drainage basin.

The different features of a drainage basin affect how quickly or slowly water moves through the drainage basin.

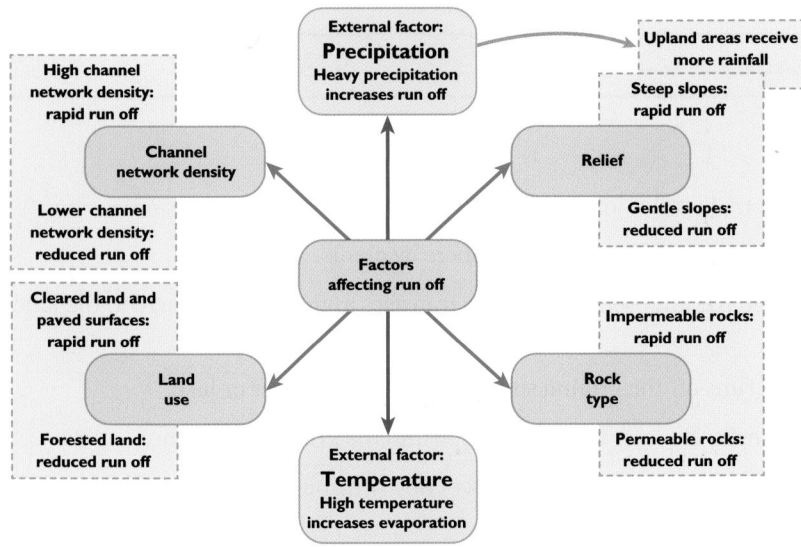

People can have little impact on drainage basin rock type or relief, but human activity can affect land use greatly, with major implications for the speed of run off in some drainage basin areas.

Figure 1.3 *Drainage basin features and external factors can all affect overland flow (run off)*

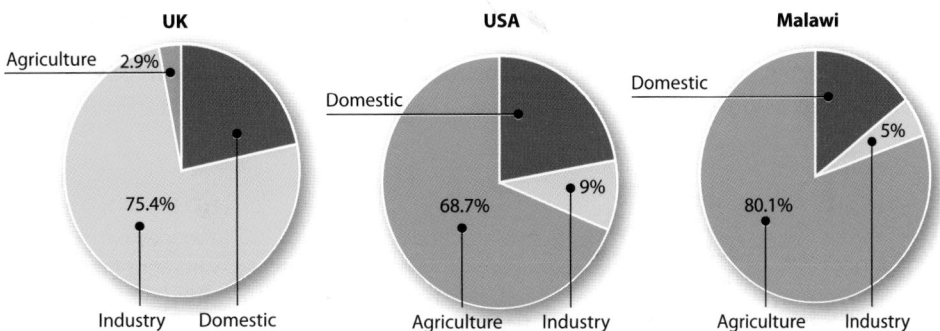

Figure 1.9 *Water use in three different countries*

Water uses, demand and supply

Water is essential for life and is used for many purposes: agriculture, industry, hygiene and sanitation, and leisure. **Figure 1.9** shows how the proportion of water that is used in homes, in industry and in agriculture changes between countries. Ninety per cent of people in Malawi farm land, so water for agriculture is very important there. Less than 1 per cent of Americans work in agriculture, but the USA uses a huge amount of water for irrigation of farmland. In the UK, industry uses most water: the majority of this is in energy production – water is used as a coolant in power stations.

Water-deficit areas are places where water demand exceeds water supply. **Water-surplus areas** are places where there is more water available than there is demand for it.

> Global demand for water has doubled every 20 years for the last 100 years.

The increase in demand comes from population growth and development. As countries develop:

- more water is used in industry (e.g. for power generation)
- more water is used in agriculture to feed growing populations
- more water is used as standards of living improve: flush toilets, showers, washing machines, etc.

Water can be transported from areas of surplus to areas of deficit, e.g. in pipelines or tankers. But water is heavy and expensive to transport.

TOP TIP

Make sure you know a case study of the rising demand for water in one country. The UK is an interesting example because population growth is happening fastest in the south and east of the country, which receives the least precipitation, while the areas of highest water supply are in the north and west.

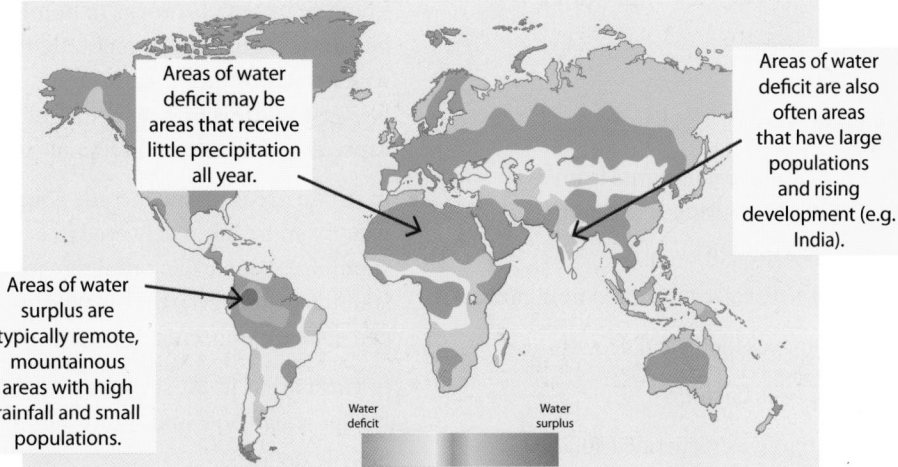

Areas of water deficit may be areas that receive little precipitation all year.

Areas of water deficit are also often areas that have large populations and rising development (e.g. India).

Areas of water surplus are typically remote, mountainous areas with high rainfall and small populations.

Water deficit

Water surplus

Figure 1.10 *Areas of water deficit and areas of water surplus*

Water quality

Water quality varies from place to place for a number of reasons. Many diseases are spread through water. If people do not have access to safe water this can have a devastating impact on their lives.

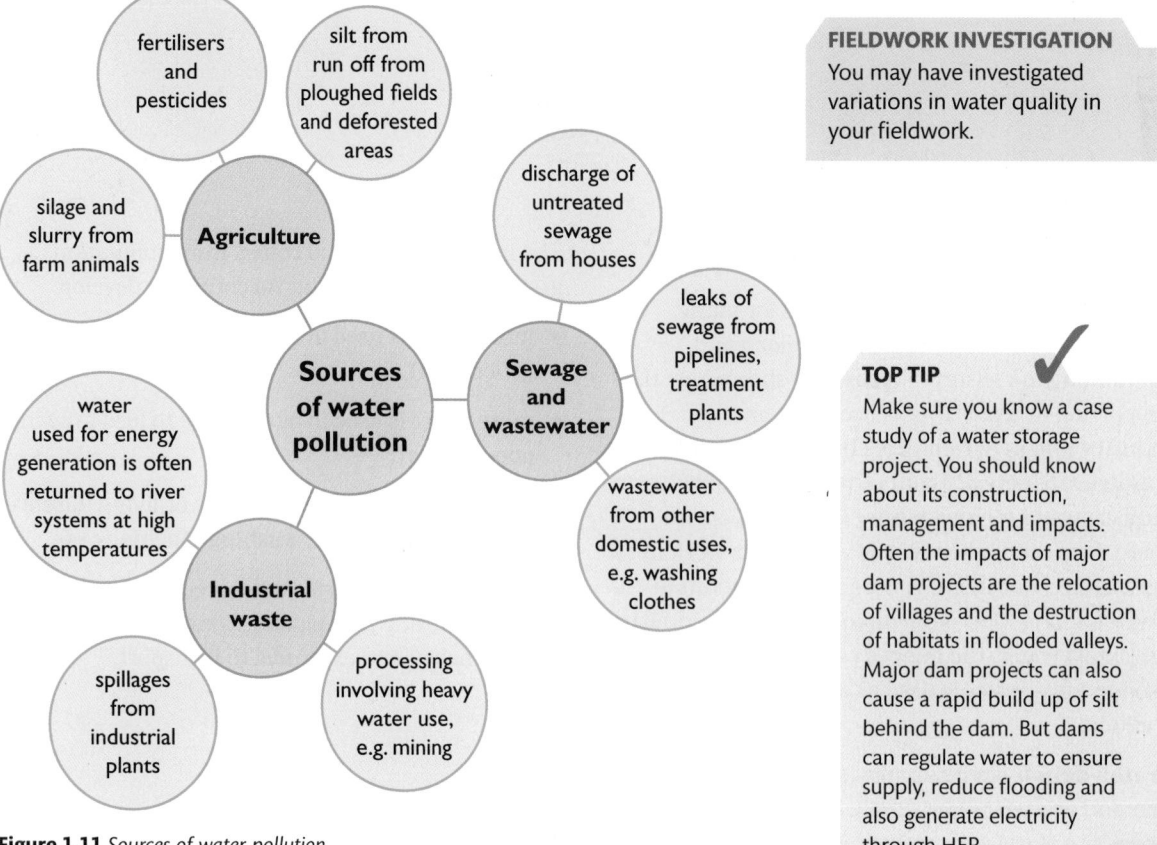

Figure 1.11 *Sources of water pollution*

FIELDWORK INVESTIGATION

You may have investigated variations in water quality in your fieldwork.

TOP TIP ✓

Make sure you know a case study of a water storage project. You should know about its construction, management and impacts. Often the impacts of major dam projects are the relocation of villages and the destruction of habitats in flooded valleys. Major dam projects can also cause a rapid build up of silt behind the dam. But dams can regulate water to ensure supply, reduce flooding and also generate electricity through HEP.

Managing the supply of clean water

The main sources of water supply are:

- rivers
- reservoirs and lakes
- aquifers and wells.

Treatment aims to remove pollutants from collected water so it is fit to drink. Treatment processes are usually combined:

- aeration – removes dissolved iron and manganese
- chlorination – removes biological growth
- disinfection – removes bacteria
- sedimentation – removes suspended solids
- filtration – removes very fine sediments.

Delivery:

- In high income countries (HICs), water delivery from the treatment works to homes and businesses is usually in pipes. By this method, water is almost never contaminated during delivery. But this infrastructure of pipes is very expensive to develop and to maintain.

- In urban areas in low income countries (LICs), water is more often delivered to a street by a standpipe. People fill containers from the standpipe and carry their water home. The water can sometimes become contaminated in this way.

- In rural areas in LICs, water usually comes from a well or water hole and is untreated. Water is often heavily polluted.

Flooding: causes and control

Flooding occurs when the amount of water moving down a river exceeds the capacity of the river's channel to hold it.

Causes

Rivers usually flood because of heavy rain or snowmelt, but the critical factor is how quickly that rainwater or meltwater reaches the river channel. The shorter the lag time (see page 3), the greater the risk that river capacity will be exceeded and flooding will occur. **Figure 1.3** (see page 2) summarises the main factors affecting this.

Human activities can make natural flooding events much worse, through deforestation, urbanisation and also through climate change, which may cause more rain and more intense precipitation.

Control

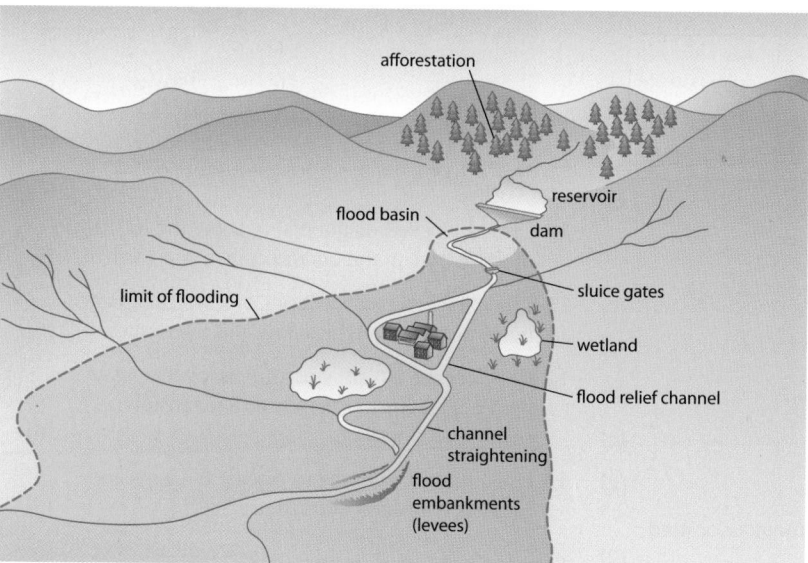

Figure 1.12 *Flood control and flood management can involve hard engineering and soft engineering strategies*

Hard engineering: the building of structures such as dams, embankments, sluice gates and flood relief channels. These structures either hold back floodwater or divert it. They are usually very expensive to construct and maintain.

Soft engineering: these methods try to avoid flood damage altogether or to minimise it. They include reforesting drainage basin slopes, or preserving marshes and wetlands on floodplains to act as temporary stores for floodwater. Urban development can be zoned also, so houses, shops and services are located on higher ground while lower ground is used for parks, car parking, etc.

Prediction: rivers are monitored carefully and defences planned according to past flood events. The problem is that flood events vary. Most control is developed to meet medium-risk threats.

1 Study **Figure 1.13**, which shows two drainage basins.

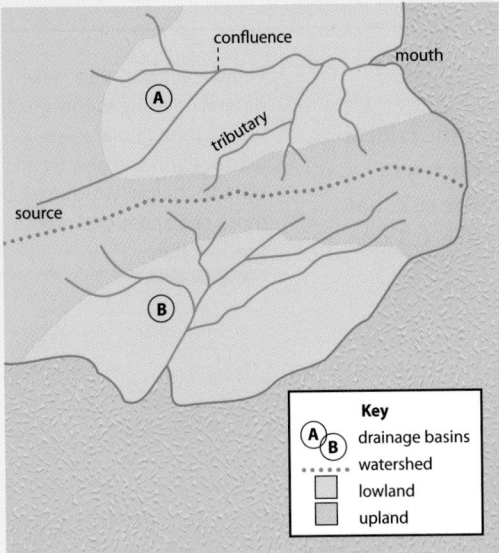

Figure 1.13

a) Which drainage basin has a more dense channel network, A or B? *(1)*

b) What is a watershed? *(1)*

2 What is the long profile of a river? *(2)*

3 What is a levee? *(2)*

4 What is an aquifer? *(2)*

5 Name **two** types of mass movement associated with river valleys. *(2)*

6 State **two** causes of water pollution. *(2)*

7 Outline **two** reasons why global water demand is increasing. *(4)*

8 Describe **two** factors that increase surface run off in a drainage basin. *(4)*

9 Study **Figure 1.14**, which shows ways in which rivers transport their load. Name the processes shown at W, X, Y and Z. *(4)*

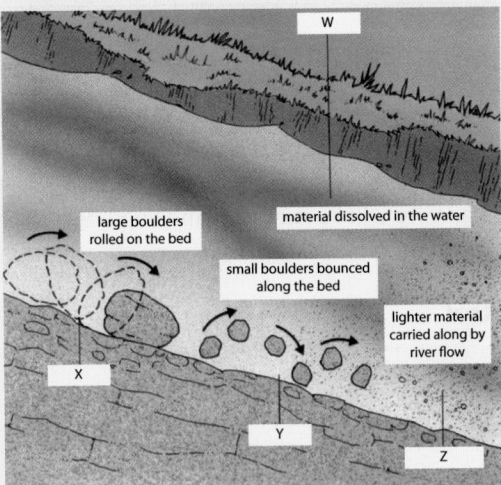

Figure 1.14

10 Draw a labelled diagram(s) to show the formation of a waterfall in the upland course of a river. *(6)*

11 Draw labelled cross sections of a typical upland river valley and a typical lowland river valley. *(6)*

12 Consider the advantages and disadvantages of hard engineering strategies as a means of controlling flooding. *(6)*

13 Use a named example to discuss the aims and impacts of a water storage project. *(9)*

Exam Section C question

14 Name **three** channel characteristics that could be investigated during fieldwork. *(3)*

Chapter 2: Coastal environments

The coast as a system

The coast is an open system. For example, sediment comes into the system (input) from a river delta. Waves transport the sediment or it is stored in beaches or sand dunes. Sediment may be lost to the coastal system if it moves into the open sea (output).

> Coastal processes are divided into **marine processes** (waves) and **sub-aerial processes** (weathering and mass movement).

Waves and erosion and deposition

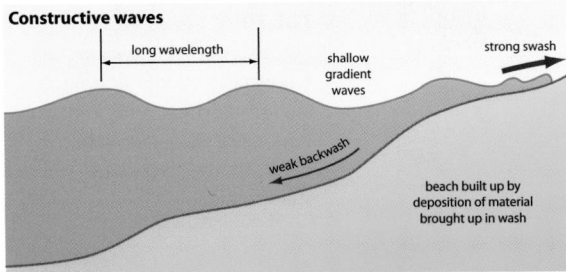
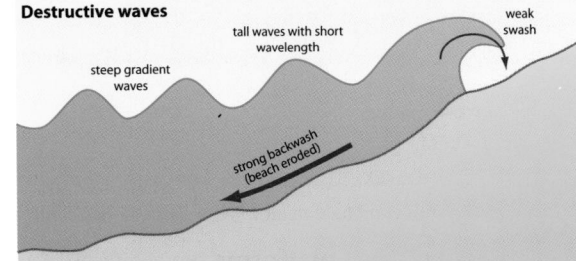

Figure 2.1 *Constructive and destructive waves*

Constructive waves build the beach by deposition. Their swash is stronger than their backwash so they carry material up the beach and deposit it there.

Destructive waves erode the beach. Their backwash is stronger than their swash, so they drag material down the beach and into the sea.

Destructive waves are responsible for most of the erosion along a coast. Four processes are involved:

1. hydraulic action – the power of the waves hitting the coast
2. abrasion – waves pick up stones and hurl them at the coast
3. corrosion – sea water gradually dissolves some rock components
4. attrition – material carried by waves bumps against other material and is worn smaller and smoother.

- Erosion at the coast is speeded up by weathering: physical, chemical and biological.
- Mass movement also provides material for wave erosion – rock falls, slumps and land slides.

Waves and transportation

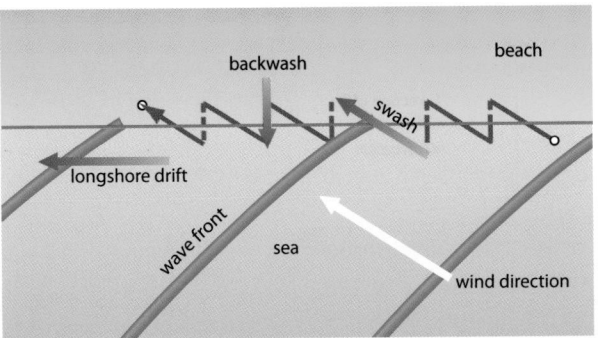

Figure 2.2 *Waves move material along the shore by longshore drift*

> **TOP TIP** ✓
> Make sure you can draw and annotate your own version of a longshore drift diagram

Coastal landforms: erosional landforms

Headlands and bays

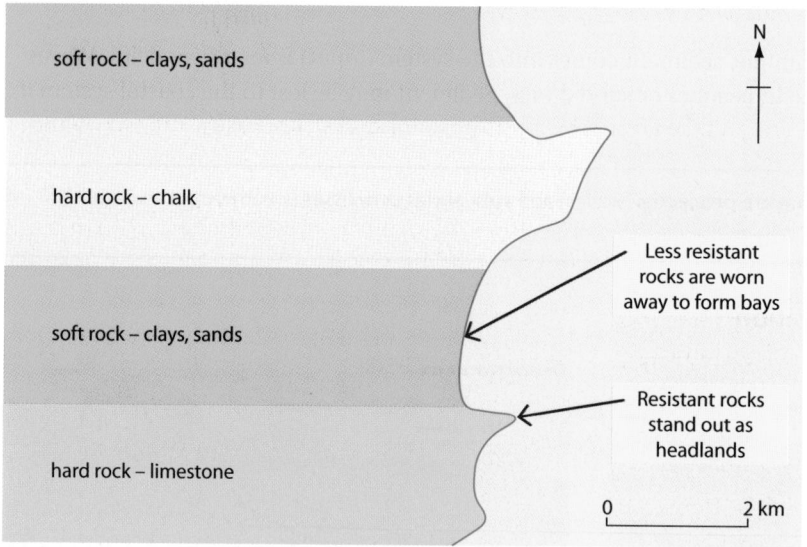

soft rock – clays, sands

hard rock – chalk

soft rock – clays, sands

Less resistant rocks are worn away to form bays

Resistant rocks stand out as headlands

hard rock – limestone

 N

0   2 km

Figure 2.3 *Headlands and bays result when a coastline has bands of more and less resistant rock*

TOP TIP ✔

Make sure you know a case study of two geologically contrasting coastlines. A common choice is between a **concordant** coastline, where the rock outcrops run parallel to the sea, and a **discordant** coastline where the rocks outcrop at right angles to the sea, forming headlands and bays.

TOP TIP ✔

Make sure you know how the following erosional landforms are formed: headlands and bays, cliffs, wave-cut platforms, caves, arches, stacks and stumps.

Cliffs and wave-cut platforms

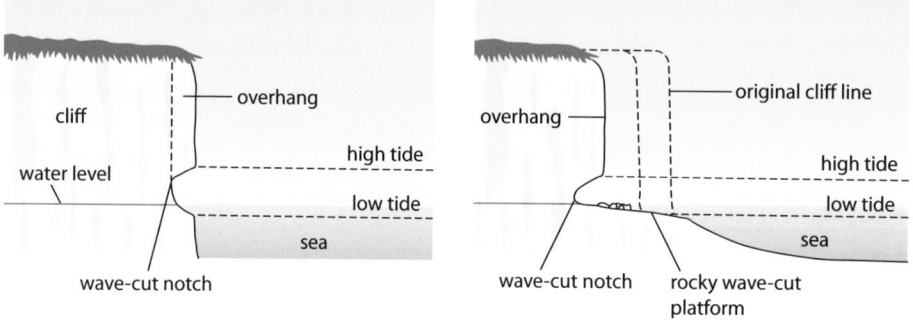

cliff

overhang

high tide

water level

low tide

sea

wave-cut notch

overhang

original cliff line

high tide

low tide

sea

wave-cut notch

rocky wave-cut platform

Figure 2.4 *The formation of cliffs and wave-cut platforms*

Caves, arches, stacks and stumps

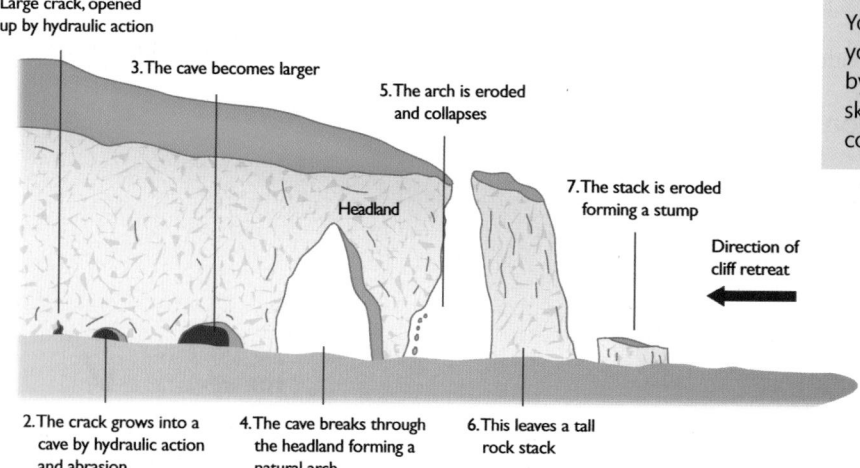

1. Large crack, opened up by hydraulic action

3. The cave becomes larger

5. The arch is eroded and collapses

7. The stack is eroded forming a stump

Headland

Direction of cliff retreat

2. The crack grows into a cave by hydraulic action and abrasion

4. The cave breaks through the headland forming a natural arch

6. This leaves a tall rock stack

Figure 2.5 *How caves, arches, stacks and stumps are formed*

PRACTICAL SKILLS

You can revise and practise your skills at the same time by drawing annotated sketches based on photos of coastal erosional landforms.

The natural environment (Section A)

Coastal landforms: depositional landforms

Depositional landforms are produced on coastlines where mud, sand and shingle accumulate faster than they can be moved away by waves.

TOP TIP

Make sure you know how the following depositional landforms are formed: beaches, spits and bars.

Beaches

Beaches are accumulations of sand and shingle formed by deposition and shaped by erosion, transportation and deposition.

Figure 2.6 *Beaches can be straight or curved. Curved beaches are formed by waves refracting as they enter a bay*

Ridges in a beach parallel to the sea are called **berms** and the one highest up the beach shows where the highest tide reaches.

Figure 2.7 *Beaches can be sandy or pebbly (shingle). Shingle beaches are usually found where cliffs are being eroded and where waves are powerful*

FIELDWORK INVESTIGATION

You may have investigated beach profiles and sediment characteristics in your fieldwork.

Spits

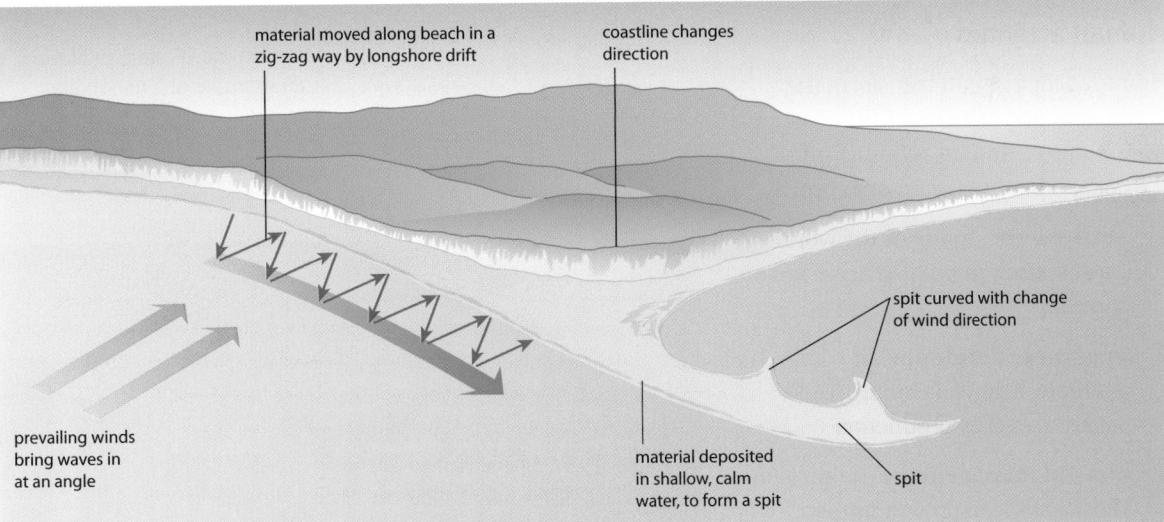

material moved along beach in a zig-zag way by longshore drift

coastline changes direction

spit curved with change of wind direction

prevailing winds bring waves in at an angle

material deposited in shallow, calm water, to form a spit

spit

Figure 2.8 *Spits are long narrow beaches of sand or shingle that are attached to the land at one end. They extend across a bay or estuary or where the coastline changes direction. They are formed by longshore drift powered by a strongly prevailing wind*

Bars

If a spit develops in a bay, it may build across it and link the two headlands to form a bar. This requires a gently sloping beach and no sizeable river entering the bay. Water trapped on the landward side of the bar forms a lagoon.

Factors affecting coasts

As well as marine and sub-aerial processes (see page 11), there are a range of other factors that affect coasts, in particular:

- geology
- vegetation
- sea-level changes
- human activities.

Geology

Where a coastline is made up of more and less resistant rocks, the less resistant rocks are eroded more than the resistant rocks. This can lead to a coastline of headlands and bays (see page 12).

Geology also affects the shape of cliffs. Hard rocks form high, rugged, steep cliffs. Softer rocks are generally less high and less steep and usually have evidence of slumping.

Vegetation

Vegetation helps to protect and preserve coastal landforms. Over time, features such as sand dunes will be colonised and 'fixed' by vegetation.

Sea-level changes

- Rising sea levels produce **submergent coastlines**, with rias (drowned river valleys) and fjords (drowned glacial valleys).

- Falling sea levels produce **emergent coastlines**, with raised beaches (old wave-cut platforms and beaches now above sea level) and relict cliffs.

Sea levels have fallen and risen many times in the past. Sea-level rises linked to global warming in the modern era would have a significant effect: many major cities are on low-lying coasts.

Human activities

Human activities can transform the landscapes and features of the coast. A wide range of human activities affect the coast. The three main ones are:

Miami in the US state of Florida is an example of a major city that is vulnerable to sea level rise. The city is built at sea level.

1. **settlement** – many of the world's most densely populated areas are on the coast

2. **economic development** – for example, fishing, farming, trade, tourism, energy production

3. **coastal management** – controlling the coastline to protect human interests.

Figure 2.9 *Downtown Miami*

Coastal ecosystems 1: coral reefs

Distribution

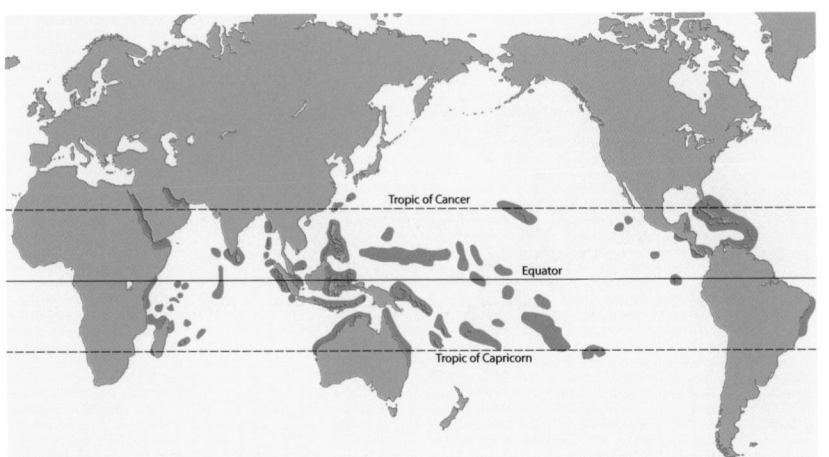

Figure 2.10 *The global distribution of coral reefs*

TOP TIP ✓

Make sure you know about four coastal **ecosystems**: **coral reefs**, **mangroves**, **sand dunes** and **salt marshes**. You need to know the physical factors that affect their distributions, their value to people and how they are under threat.

Make sure you know a case study of one coastal ecosystem.

Coral reefs are huge deposits of calcium carbonate built up entirely by marine organisms. Key factors control their distribution:

Minimum water temperature of 18°C	Sea less than 25 m deep – plenty of light	Salt water	Clear, clean water – sediment blocks light
✓	✓	✓	✓

Value

- **Biodiversity** – the Great Barrier Reef, for example, has 700 species of coral, 1500 species of fish, 4000 species of mollusc.
- Coral reefs soak up wave energy and so help to protect low-lying coasts from tropical storms.
- Fishing – coral reefs support many people in LICs.
- Tourism – more than 150 million people a year visit areas with coral reefs.

Threats

A survey in 2012 showed that only 8% of reefs in the Caribbean had live coral cover, compared with more than 50% in the 1970s.

Coral reefs are delicately balanced ecosystems and are easily stressed by human activities. The following activities pose particular threats:

- pollution
- overfishing
- quarrying of coral for building stone
- warming sea temperatures – this causes coral bleaching.

Any water pollution that blocks light threatens corals, for example silt from land clearance, algal blooms caused by fertiliser run off, increased sediment from sewage outflows. Tourist developments near coral reefs can damage the very thing tourists have come to see.

St Lucia in the Caribbean is a good example of how coral reefs have been protected by coastal management zoning.

Coastal ecosystems 2: mangroves

Distribution

TOP TIP ✔

Make sure you know a case study of one coastal ecosystem. The Sundarbans in Bangladesh is a good example of a mangrove ecosystem.

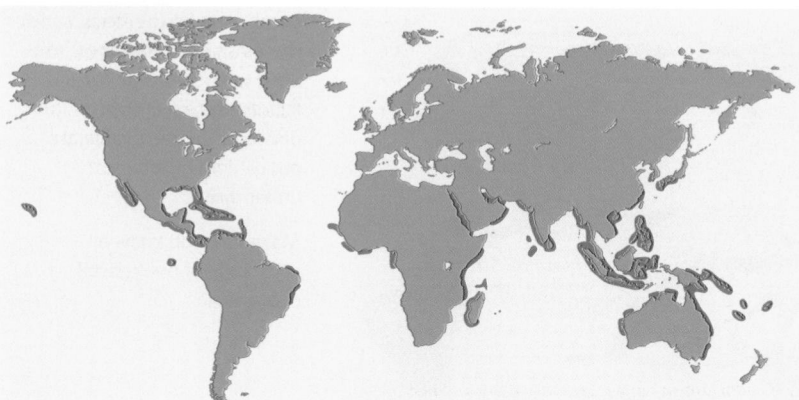

Figure 2.11 *The global distribution of mangroves*

Mangroves are most common in South-East Asia, and most are now found within 30° latitude of the Equator. Mangroves grow in the intertidal zone so they need to be able to cope with a very dynamic environment:

- mangroves have a filtration system to cope with salt water
- some species have snorkel-like roots so they can take in air when submerged by mud, the tide or by coastal flooding
- some species have prop roots or buttress roots that keep them stable in the soft mud of the intertidal zone
- mangroves have floating seeds, which are transported by the waves to start new mangroves.

Value

- Biodiversity – mangroves are rich in wildlife and act as nurseries for many fish species.
- The complex root systems of mangroves trap sediment and eventually build up the intertidal zone into land.
- They soak up wave energy so help protect low-lying coasts from tropical storms.
- Mangroves provide fuel and building material.

> Death tolls from the 2004 tsunami were often higher in coastal areas that had cleared mangroves than those that still had mangroves along their coast.

Threats

Mangroves are most threatened by economic development.

- Shrimp and fish aquaculture is a boom industry in much of coastal South-East Asia and has involved large-scale clearance of mangroves.
- Mangroves are felled for timber and fuel, and their deforestation clears land for development.

Bangladesh's Coastal Zone Policy involves planting mangroves to protect the low-lying country from storm surges and also to reclaim land. 1,290,000 hectares of new land have been reclaimed by using mangroves to trap sediments and stabilise shores.

Coastal ecosystems 3: salt marshes and sand dunes

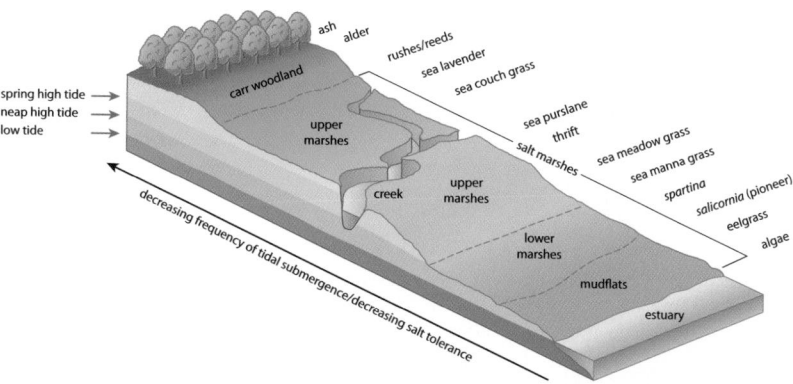

Figure 2.12 *Salt marsh zones: the frequency of tidal submergence and the level of salinity determine which plants and animals are found in each zone*

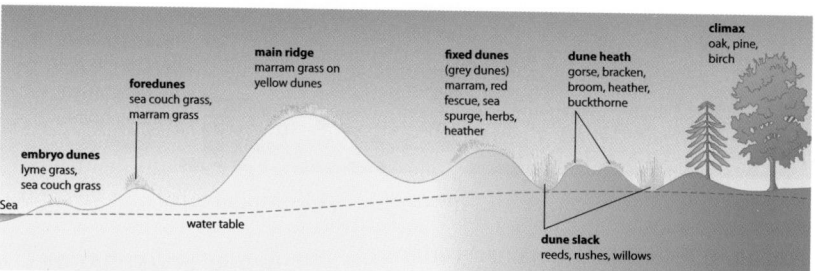

Figure 2.13 *A cross-section through a typical sand dune ecosystem. Over time, the ridges of dunes are colonised and 'fixed' by vegetation*

Colonising plants in a sand dune ecosystem need to be able to deal with salinity, a lack of moisture because sand drains quickly, wind, and being covered by windblown sand.

Value

Salt marsh is often drained and reclaimed for farmland or for development but its greatest value is now recognised as a means of coastal defence: the creeks and vegetation slow waves down and reduce the impact of coastal flooding, as well as providing a buffer against coastal erosion. Salt marshes are also a key habitat for wildlife, especially wading birds.

Sand dunes are involved in the colonisation of land from the intertidal zone and they also have great recreational value.

Threats

- Salt marsh is threatened by development, but also by agricultural and industrial pollution and, most of all, by rising sea levels.

- Sand dunes are not really under threat. But there are issues with over-use of dunes for recreation, causing a loss of vegetation and the 'blow out' of the dune.

The natural environment (Section A)

Coastal conflicts

Conflicts between coastal users are referred to as conflicts between **stakeholders**: people with different interests in the coast.

local residents want clean environment, jobs, affordable housing

employers want space to build shops, offices, factories

developers want new sites by the sea for tourist developments

transport companies want well-connected ports and terminals

fishermen want harbours, unpolluted waters, protection from competition

farmers want well-drained land, shelter from sea winds

government wants to build offshore wind farms

tourists want beaches, hotels, entertainment, holiday homes, marinas

Figure 2.14 *Coastal stakeholders*

As **Figure 2.15** shows, it is very difficult to reconcile both conservation and development of the coastal environment. Coastal managers often seek to separate the two, but the impacts of development are often far-reaching.

The needs of different coastal stakeholders can often conflict with one another as they all compete for the same resources. A conflict matrix is a good way of analysing these conflicts.

FIELDWORK INVESTIGATION
You may have investigated the conflicts between development and conservation on a stretch of coastline as part of a fieldwork investigation.

Activity	Conservation of the natural environment	Port and harbour operation	Extracting gravel from sea bed	Fishing	Economic development	Shipping	Wind and wave farms	Beach recreation
Conservation of the natural environment								
Port and harbour operation								
Extracting gravel from sea bed								
Fishing								
Economic development								
Shipping								
Wind and wave farms								
Beach recreation								

Key: ▢ No conflict or little conflict   ▢ Some conflict   ▢ Strong conflict   ▢ Very strong conflict

Figure 2.15 *An example of a conflict matrix for coastal users*

Coastal management

Coastal management is fundamentally concerned with managing the risks associated with coastal erosion and/or the risks associated with coastal flooding. Rising sea levels significantly increase the risks of both.

> The northeast coastline of Britain has coastal erosion rates of between 1 m and 10 m per year. This is due to the combination of soft rocks exposed to powerful destructive waves.

Coastal management strategies

- **Hard engineering** methods involve building some type of sea defence.
- **Soft engineering** methods try to work with natural processes to reduce the impact of erosion or flooding.

TOP TIP ✓

Make sure you know a case study of a retreating coastline – causes, impacts and management. A popular UK example is the Holderness coast (see Key fact, left). The village of Mappleton on the Holderness coast has a population of around 100, and has been protected from rapid erosion by two rock groynes and a stretch of rip-rap, at the cost of £2 million. While Mappleton has been protected, erosion may have been made worse elsewhere down the coast.

Strategy	Description	Advantages	Disadvantages
Hard engineering			
Sea wall	A wall, often made of concrete, which protects the coast from waves	Prevents both erosion and flooding (if high enough)	Very expensive to build and to maintain. Obtrusive to look at
Groynes	Wood or steel piling built at right angles to the beach that traps beach material being moved by longshore drift	Slows beach erosion, creates wide beach	Starves beaches downstream of sediment, increasing erosion
Rip-rap	Large boulders piled up to protect a stretch of coast	Cheaper to construct than sea walls and does similar job of absorbing wave energy	Boulders can be undercut and be dislodged in heavy storms
Soft engineering			
Beach replenishment	Pumping or dumping sand and shingle back onto a beach to replace eroded material	Beaches absorb wave energy and help protect against coastal erosion	Has to be repeated often, which is expensive
Fencing, hedging and replacing vegetation	Helps stabilise sand dunes or beaches and reduces wind erosion	A relatively cheap way to protect against flooding and erosion	Hard to protect larger areas of coastline this way
Cliff regrading	The angle of a cliff is reduced to reduce mass movement	Prevents sudden loss of large sections of cliff	Doesn't prevent wave erosion of the cliffs
Managed retreat			
Managed retreat	Abandoning existing coastal defences and allowing the sea to flood inland until it reaches higher land or a new line of sea defences	No expensive construction costs; creates salt marsh – a valuable habitat	Often very unpopular with people threatened by coastal erosion or flooding

There are conflicting views about the value of hard engineering or soft engineering approaches. Most coastal managers aim to use a range of methods depending on the value of what is being protected.

1 Study **Figure 2.16**, a map of the Holderness coast, England.

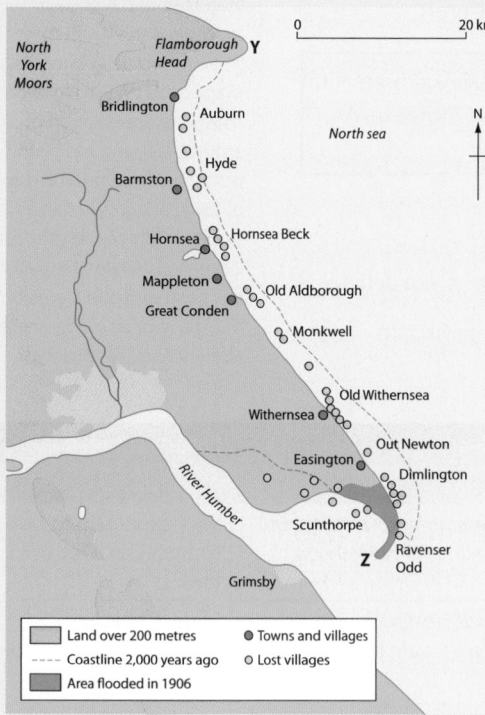

Figure 2.16

Map legend:
- Land over 200 metres
- ---- Coastline 2,000 years ago
- Area flooded in 1906
- ● Towns and villages
- ○ Lost villages

a) What marine process is responsible for the retreat of the Holderness coast? *(1)*

b) What is the coastal landform at point Y: a bay, a headland or a concordant coast? *(1)*

c) What is the name of the coastal landform at point Z: a spit, a bar or a stack? *(1)*

2 What is managed retreat? *(2)*

3 Name **two** of the four main wave erosion processes. *(2)*

4 Name **two** landforms formed by coastal erosion. *(2)*

5 Name **two** landforms formed by coastal deposition. *(2)*

6 Explain the difference between swash and backwash. *(2)*

7 Use an annotated sketch or sketches to describe how a destructive wave erodes a beach. *(4)*

8 Use an annotated sketch to show how longshore drift transports material along the coastline. *(4)*

9 Describe **two** ways in which human activity can harm a coral reef ecosystem. *(4)*

10 Explain the difference between hard engineering and soft engineering methods of coastal management. *(4)*

11 Describe the advantages and disadvantages of using a 'do nothing' approach to coastal erosion. *(6)*

12 Describe the value to humans of **either** coral reefs **or** mangroves. *(6)*

13 Using a named example, describe the impacts that a retreating coastline can have on people's lives. *(9)*

Exam Section C question

14 Briefly describe how a quadrat could be used to collect pebble measurements in a vertical transect up a beach. *(3)*

Chapter 3: Hazardous environments

Different types of hazard

Make sure you know and understand these key terms:

- **Hazard**: an event resulting from environmental processes that threatens or actually causes damage and destruction to people, their property and settlements.

- **Natural disaster**: when a hazard causes serious damage and destruction.

> For a disaster to be listed on the International Disaster Database, one of the following criteria needs to be met:
> - 10 people or more are killed
> - 100 people or more are injured
> - a state of emergency is declared
> - a call for international assistance is made.

Hazards can be put into categories according to their causes:

Geological	Climatic	Biological	Technological
Earthquakes	Storms	Fires	Nuclear explosion
Volcanic eruptions	Floods	Pests	Accidents
Landslides	Drought	Diseases	Pollution

- Sometimes hazards combine to create events, for example lava from a volcanic eruption can block a river which causes a flood.

- Some hazards have human causes or are made more hazardous by human activity.

> This topic focuses on three tectonic and climatic hazards: **volcanoes**, **earthquakes** and **tropical storms**.

Hazards and disasters

Hazards are a threat to people but not all of them become disasters. Whether they do depends on different factors:

- **Scale and type** – not all hazards are equally hazardous. For example, some types of volcanoes have explosive eruptions while others do not.

- **Distribution and frequency** – some places are more hazardous than others. Some hazards occur more frequently than others. Rare events are hard to predict and prepare for.

- **Human response** – the readiness and ability of people in an area to absorb and recover from the effects of a natural hazard. There are often crucial differences in response between HICs and LICs.

Earthquakes

Earthquakes are tectonic hazards.

Global distribution

The distribution of earthquakes closely follows the margins of the world's tectonic plates.

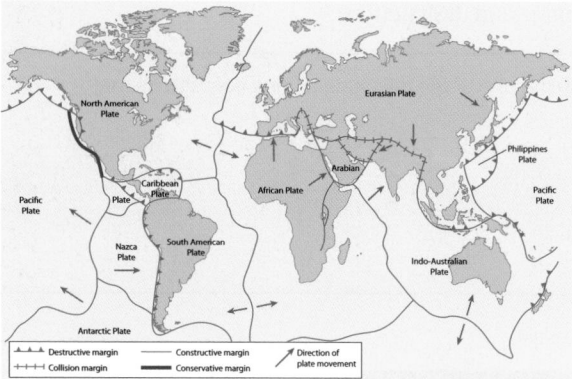

Figure 3.1 *The crust of the Earth is made up of a number of tectonic plates. Their movements result in four different types of plate margin*

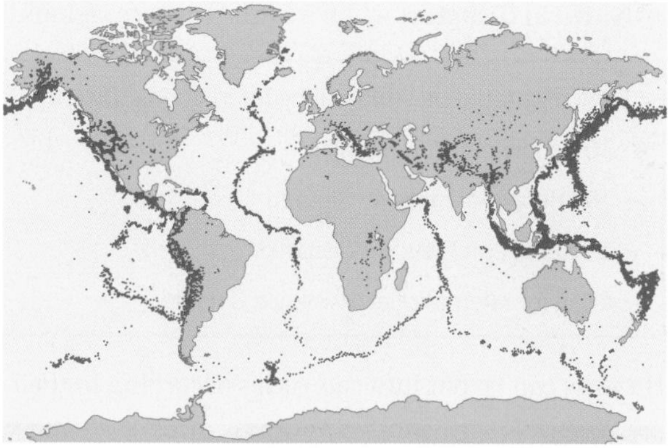

Figure 3.2 *Global distribution of earthquakes*

Causes

While earthquakes are associated with all types of plate margin, they are more frequent at:

- **destructive margins** – where one plate margin is being destroyed as it plunges beneath another plate

- **conservative margins** – where two plates slide past each other.

Characteristics

An earthquake is a sudden and brief period of intense ground-shaking. The ground movement can be both vertical and horizontal.

- The centre of the earthquake underground is called the **focus**.

- The point on the surface above the focus is the **epicentre**.

- The amount of damage caused by the earthquake depends on the depth of the focus and the type of rock. The worst damage happens when the focus is close to the surface and the rocks are soft.

- Earthquakes under the sea can produce tsunamis.

The strength of an earthquake is measured on two different scales:

The **Richter scale** measures energy released by an earthquake. It is measured on a seismograph. The Richter scale is a logarithmic scale that runs up to 8. Each point up on the scale represents 30 times more energy released than the point below.

The **Mercalli scale** is based on what people experience and the amount of damage done. People would not even feel the tremor at 2 on the Mercalli scale. However, at 5 on the scale household things fall over, at 10–12 houses collapse, there are landslides and the ground cracks.

Volcanoes

Volcanoes are tectonic hazards.

Global distribution

The distribution of volcanoes closely follows the margins of the world's tectonic plates. Compare this map of volcano distribution with **Figure 3.1** on the previous page.

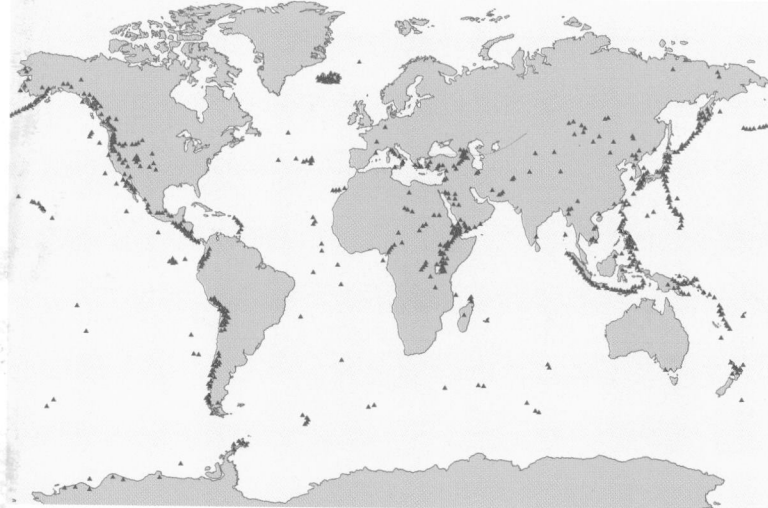

PRACTICAL SKILLS

Practise your map skills by mapping the location of recent earthquakes, volcanoes and tropical storms.

Figure 3.3 *Global distribution of volcanoes*

Causes

Like earthquakes, volcanoes mostly occur at plate margins. There are also **hotspot** volcanoes, which form in the middle of plates as the plates move over a plume of magma.

Characteristics

- Volcanoes formed at constructive margins have more gentle, regular and frequent eruptions.
- Volcanoes formed at destructive margins are much more violent, infrequent and irregular. That makes them more dangerous to people living near them.

There are several different hazards associated with volcanic eruptions.

- **Lava flows** destroy everything they move over, but they rarely extend for more than 10 km from a volcano.
- **Ash** can be carried for hundreds of miles in the atmosphere. Close to a volcano where the ash is thickest, it can choke people and animals and form such thick layers that it causes roofs to collapse.
- **Pyroclastic flows** are superheated clouds of gas and rocks that sweep down the volcano sides. As the clouds can be up to 1000°C and travel at 450 miles per hour, they are extremely hazardous.
- **Tsunamis** can be caused by volcanic eruptions.

Tropical storms

Tropical storms are climatic hazards.

Global distribution

The distribution of tropical storms is limited by temperature, because sea water temperatures must be more than 27°C for them to form. This also means they tend to occur in mid summer and early autumn when sea temperatures are at their warmest.

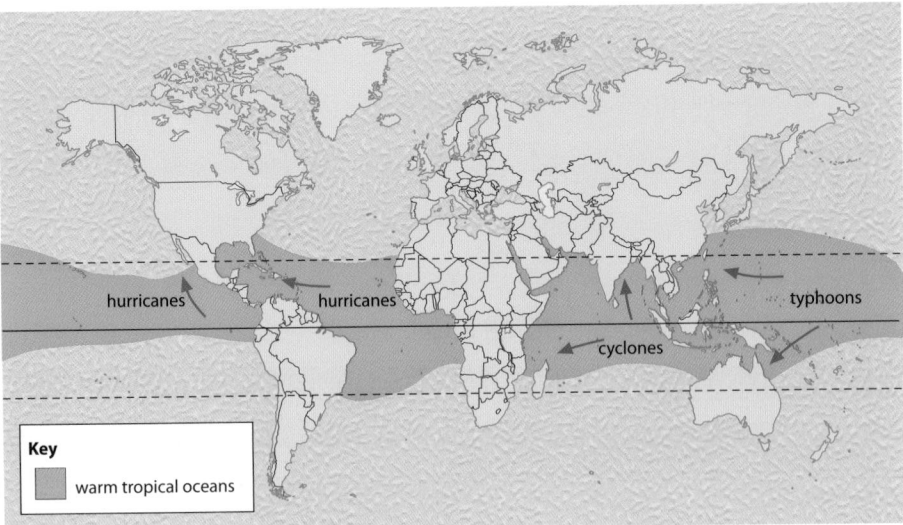

Figure 3.4 *Global distribution of tropical storms. Tropical storms have different names in different parts of the world*

Causes

Tropical storms develop in five main stages:

1. Warm, moist air rises and condenses, releasing huge amounts of energy. This powers the storm.

2. As the air rises it sucks in more warm moist air behind it.

3. The air spirals upwards rapidly, which causes high winds.

4. The water vapour in the air condenses as it rises and cools, forming huge clouds and heavy rain.

5. The cool and dry air falls in the centre of the storm, forming the eye.

Characteristics

- Tropical storms move westwards because winds blow from the east around the equator.
- They lose strength on land because they are powered by warm sea water.
- The eye is the centre of the storm. Here there are light winds and no clouds or rain.
- The eyewall or vortex surrounds the eye. Here the air is rapidly spiralling upwards, causing high winds (between 55 and 118 km/h), torrential rain and storm clouds.
- At the edges of the hurricane conditions are less intense. Here it is rainy, windy and cloudy.

Tropical storms cause wind damage but the huge waves they generate also lead to storm surges and coastal flooding. Torrential rain can lead to landslides.

Methods of monitoring weather conditions

As tropical storms and other climatic hazards develop under certain conditions and move from one area to another, it is important that they are tracked and forecasted.

Data sources

Meteorologists measure and monitor weather conditions using different sources of data.

- **Weather stations** – a global network of weather stations monitor weather conditions. These data are used for forecasting and also tracking tropical storms.

- **Weather satellites** allow meteorologists to see and analyse pictures of cloud formations from images captured during the day. Satellite sensors also monitor energy radiations, which can be captured day or night.

- **Radar** provides important information on the direction and speed that clouds are moving and allows meteorologists to gauge precipitation.

FIELDWORK INVESTIGATION
You may have investigated weather conditions and how they are monitored as part of your fieldwork.

Classification

Tropical storms range in severity and they often develop in intensity as they track over an area of ocean. **Figure 3.5** shows the Saffir-Simpson classification of tropical storms.

Category	Wind speed (kph)	Pressure (mb)	Storm surge (m)	Damage
1	119–153	>980	1.0–1.7	Minor – trees, mobile homes
2	154–177	979–965	1.8–2.6	Roofs and windows of buildings Small boats broken from moorings Flooding
3	178–209	964–945	2.7–3.8	Structural damage to buildings Flooding over 1 m up to 10 km inland
4	210–249	944–920	3.9–5.6	Major – destroys buildings, beaches and floods up to 10 km inland
5	>250	<920	>5.7	Catastrophic – destruction up to 5 m above sea level Mass evacuation needed
Note that tropical storms have wind speeds between 55 and 118 km/h.				

Figure 3.5 *The Saffir-Simpson classification of tropical storms*

Prediction

Monitoring and classifying a tropical storm as it develops can help to warn people in the path of the storm about what conditions are coming their way. This allows people to make appropriate preparations, depending on the options available to them. These options are often very different in HICs compared with many LICs.

The scale and impacts of natural disasters

The impact of a natural disaster depends on many factors, including:

- the scale of the event: area affected, energy released, duration of event
- how much warning people have
- how prepared people are for this kind of disaster
- the density of population in the areas affected
- the ability of a country to respond quickly and cope effectively with the disaster.

Disasters have different impacts in LICs and HICs because:

- HICs are better prepared
- HICs are better able to respond quickly and effectively.

HICs can do this because they have more money and better technology.

TOP TIP

Make sure you know a case study that you can use to compare the impacts of a natural disaster in an **HIC** and in an **LIC**.

TOP TIP

You may have studied different case studies from the ones compared here: make sure you revise the studies you did at school as these will have the level of detail you need.

The natural environment (Section A)

Tropical storm in poor country

Date: 2 May 2008
Name and location: Cyclone Nargis, Myanmar

Storm details: Winds up to 215 km/h, high winds, heavy rain and storm surges. Irrawaddy Delta region particularly affected.

Effects

- Social: at least 140,000 dead, up to 3 million homeless, 95 per cent of homes destroyed.
- Economic: US$10 billion was needed to rebuild homes and clear transport routes.
- Environmental: drinking water polluted, diseases spread, farmland damaged by salt

Responses

- Storm was tracked by Bangladesh but Myanmar's government did not warn its population.
- Short-term responses: UN launched a huge appeal for aid to Myanmar but the government was reluctant to let foreign organisations help.
- Long-term responses: Myanmar is still relying on foreign aid to rebuild and recovery is slow.

Tropical storm in rich country

Date: 29 August 2005
Name and location: Hurricane Katrina, USA

Storm details: Category 3 hurricane, winds up to 280 km/h, 8.5 m high storm surge that punched through levee defences of New Orleans and caused widespread flooding.

Effects

- Social: 1836 dead, 1 million homeless, lack of clean water and sanitation, problems with looting and social disorder.
- Economic: US$98 billion to rebuild housing, care for people made homeless and jobless.
- Environmental: coastal habitats damaged, floodwaters polluted.

Responses

- State of emergency declared two days before the storm made landfall.
- National Guard mobilised, emergency shelters set up, evacuations took place in many cities.
- Massive effort to rescue survivors and provide shelter and support for the homeless.
- Long-term responses: rebuilding and strengthening of flood defences and the major rebuilding of New Orleans.

Figure 3.6 *Comparing impacts of tropical storms in a LIC and a HIC*

Reasons for living in high-risk areas

Comparing **Figure 3.7**, a map of population densities by country, with the maps on previous pages of the distribution of earthquakes, volcanoes and tropical storms shows that people do not avoid living in areas with a higher risk of natural disaster.

Key

0–10
10–25
25–50
50–75
75–100
100–150
150–300
300–1000
1000+

● cities with populations greater than 5 million

Figure 3.7 *Population density (number of people per km²) by country, 2006, and cities with populations greater than 5 million*

Why do so many people continue to live and work in what are clearly hazardous areas?

- Disasters might be quite rare, so people either think that it will never happen again or they are not sufficiently educated to know how likely it is that it will happen again.

- There may be other benefits to living in the area that outweigh the risks – for example, very fertile soil from volcanic ash, geothermal energy, tourism, rich alluvial soils in frequently flooded areas.

- People may not be able to move away because they don't have the money or job prospects to move.

- People may believe they will not be affected or they may be fatalistic and think that what happens will happen, regardless of what they do.

- Population densities have built up over centuries and large areas of population, especially big cities, have many advantages that keep them growing.

Mitigating the consequences of hazards: predicting and preparing

Mitigating the consequences of hazards involves taking actions before, during and after the event.

Predicting hazards

Volcanoes

Some indications that an eruption may be imminent can be monitored by special (and expensive) equipment:

- an increase in the number of small earthquakes before an eruption
- a swelling may develop on the side of the volcano
- gases, such as sulphur dioxide, may escape.

Figure 3.8 *Volcano monitoring equipment at the edge of the crater of Mount Vesuvius*

Earthquakes

Most earthquakes happen without any warning at all. In a few cases:

- there are very small changes in electrical and radioactive emissions
- land may rise or tilt
- the water level in wells may fall.

Tropical storms

Meteorologists can monitor data on tropical storms as they develop (see page 25) and can track them as they approach land. However, predicting exactly where storms will go is not easy.

Preparing for hazards

Volcanoes

- Early warning systems to aid in evacuation.
- Sloping roofs on buildings to avoid build up of ash.

Earthquakes

Earthquakes are the most difficult hazards to predict, but they can be prepared for by:

- building earthquake-proof buildings and structures (e.g. expressways)
- education – carrying out earthquake drills so everyone knows what to do
- having fully trained and equipped emergency services for an effective response
- setting up early warning systems for tsunamis.

Tropical storms

- Early warning systems to aid in evacuation.
- Preparation of storm shelters.
- Houses equipped with storm shutters to protect glass.
- Effective levees/flood protection measures to combat storm surges.

TOP TIP ✓

Make sure you know a case study of the management of a tectonic event and a case study of the management of either river flooding or coastal flooding. Earthquake preparation in a country such as Japan would be a good example.

Hurricane Katrina provides good examples of preparation for a tropical storm (80% of New Orleans' population was evacuated), and also where preparations were not sufficient to prevent disaster (1800 of those who were not evacuated died).

Mitigating the consequences of hazards: consequences of hazards

Hazards have **short-term** consequences and **longer-term** consequences.

Short-term consequences (primary impacts) of a volcanic eruption could include:

- people injured or killed
- buildings and farmland destroyed
- communications disrupted.

The longer-term consequences (secondary impacts) of the eruption could include:

- the economic costs of rebuilding
- economic slump because tourists stay away.

Responses to hazards can also be short-term and long-term:

- short-term: coping with the hazard itself, emergency **aid** and **disaster relief**
- long-term: rebuilding, review and adjustment, improving prediction and preparation.

> **TOP TIP** ✔
>
> Make sure you know a case study of the management of a tectonic event and a case study of the management of either river flooding or coastal flooding. Make sure you know relevant detail about consequences and responses

---

Named example: Asian tsunami, December 2004

In Banda Aceh, the first area to be hit, hospitals could not cope with the numbers of people injured. Immediately after the tsunami, there were so many bodies that emergency services quickly ran out of body bags. Mass graves were dug. The bodies had to be buried quickly so that disease would not spread.

← Emergency aid. Often disaster areas are hard to reach: they may be remote, or roads may be destroyed. LICs may not have the funds for helicopters.

There was a massive international response to the disaster, raising $14 billion. This funded the world's biggest ever emergency relief effort. Many different organisations coordinated their efforts to get aid to the survivors as quickly as they could, using helicopters and boats.

← Disaster relief. International organisations can raise huge sums and use their experience to coordinate relief efforts.

Since 2004, The Disasters Emergency Committee has spent £40 million on rebuilding projects in Sri Lanka and Indonesia. A new Indian Ocean tsunami warning system became operational in 2006, so that warning of future tsunamis can be given.

← Rebuilding, improving prediction and preparation. It can take decades for LICs to recover from a natural disaster. International aid agencies may make long-term commitments to rebuilding.

1 Study **Figure 3.9**, which shows the path taken by a natural hazard event.

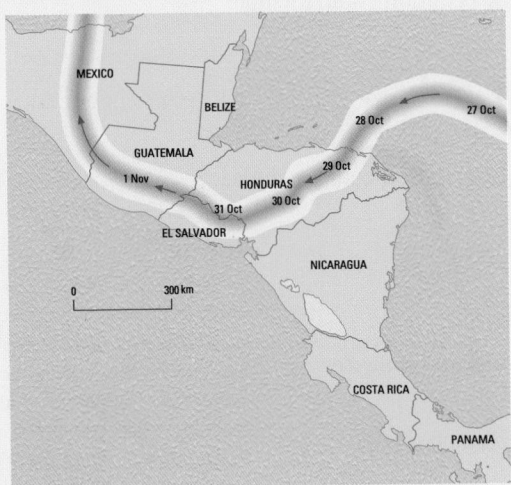

Figure 3.9

a) What type of natural hazard is being tracked in **Figure 3.9**? *(1)*

b) How many days did it take this hazard to move through Honduras, El Salvador and Guatemala, according to **Figure 3.9**? *(1)*

c) Name **one** source of data that allowed meteorologists to track this hazard. *(1)*

2 What is meant by the term 'natural hazard'? *(2)*

3 Study **Figure 3.3** on page 23, which shows the global distribution of volcanoes. Is the following statement about this distribution **true** or **false**: Volcanoes are only found on destructive plate margins. *(2)*

4 What is the epicentre of an earthquake? *(2)*

5 Name **two** hazards associated with volcanic eruptions. *(2)*

6 What is the difference between primary effects and secondary effects of a natural hazard? *(2)*

7 Describe **two** hazards that can occur when tropical revolving storms reach inhabited coastlines. *(4)*

8 Explain why people live near volcanoes despite the dangers of eruptions. *(4)*

9 Using an example, describe the impact of a major earthquake on people and property in a LIC. *(6)*

10 Using an example, describe the immediate relief efforts after an earthquake in a HIC. *(6)*

11 Explain why some volcanoes cause more damage and loss of life than others. *(6)*

12 Compare how prediction, protection and preparation differed in the responses to named tropical storms in a HIC and a LIC. *(9)*

13 Discuss the reasons why the impacts of earthquakes are normally more severe in LICs. Examples will help your answer. *(9)*

Exam Section C question

14 What factors should be considered when choosing sites around a school to measure local climatic variations? *(3)*

Chapter 4: Economic activity and energy

Economic activities and sectors

All economic activities produce something for consumption (sale) and they all create jobs. Economic activities are divided into four sectors:

- **primary sector** – working natural resources. Main activities are farming, forestry, fishing, mining and quarrying
- **secondary sector** – processing raw materials, making things by manufacturing, assembling or building
- **tertiary sector** – providing services *teachers*
- **quaternary sector** – concerned with information, research, technology.

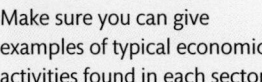

TOP TIP
Make sure you can give examples of typical economic activities found in each sector.

Broadly speaking, **LICs** depend on their primary sector, **MICs** on their secondary sector and **HICs** on their tertiary sector. The quaternary sector is a recent development in HICs.

Changes over time and space

The importance of each sector to the economy of a country changes as the country develops. This is called **sectoral shift**. Where and when this happens also varies within countries and between countries.

The UK was the first country in the world to move from an economy based on primary production (agriculture) to one based on the secondary sector. **Figure 4.1** shows the sectoral shifts involved.

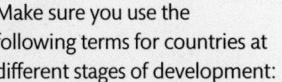

TOP TIP
Make sure you use the following terms for countries at different stages of development:

LICs – low income countries

MICs – lower and upper middle income countries

HICs – high income countries

The primary sector declined as agriculture was modernised and agricultural workers left farming for jobs in industry. Numbers employed in agriculture have continued to fall as the UK imports more food and agribusiness is increasingly mechanised.

The secondary sector has declined as things that used to be made in the UK can now be made more cheaply elsewhere in the world.

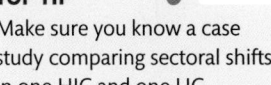

TOP TIP
Make sure you know a case study comparing sectoral shifts in one HIC and one LIC.

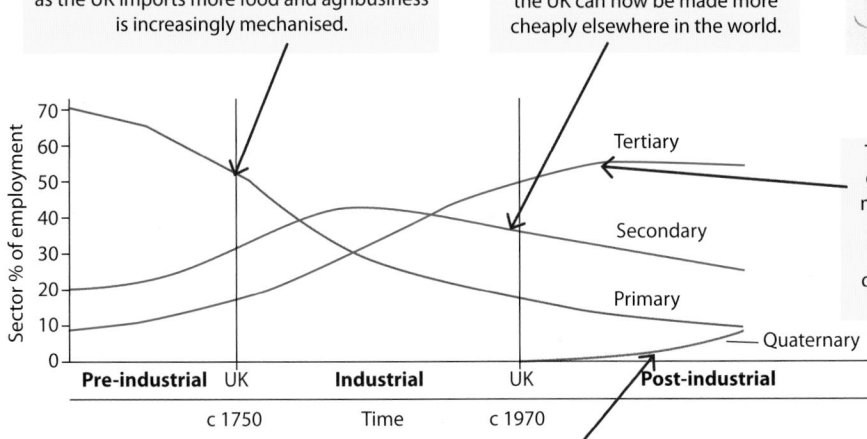

The tertiary sector develops with growing prosperity: people have more disposable income to spend on entertainment, and taxes are used to provide the services a developed nation demands for its citizens.

Figure 4.1 *Economic sector shifts in the UK*

Quaternary activities develop when countries decide to invest in cutting-edge technologies in order to stay ahead of other countries climbing the 'development ladder'.

Representing sector data

The relative importance of each sector to the economy as a whole is usually measured as a percentage of GDP (gross domestic product) or GNI (gross national income), or as a percentage of the total workforce employed by each sector.

These data can be represented in different ways. Here are just a few:

As a pie chart:

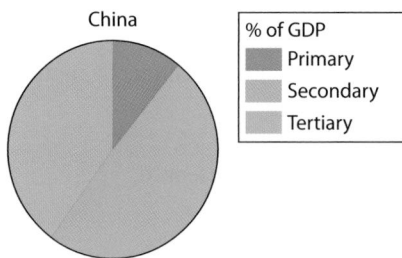

Figure 4.2 *China's economic sectors (per cent of GDP)*

As a compound bar chart:

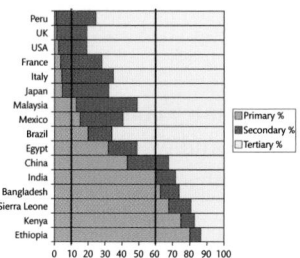

Figure 4.3 *Comparison of different countries by percentage employed per sector*

As a triangular graph:

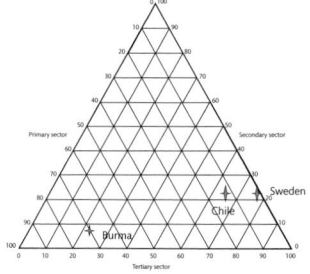

Figure 4.4 *Triangular graph comparing percentage employed per sector for three countries*

As a line graph (good for showing change over time):

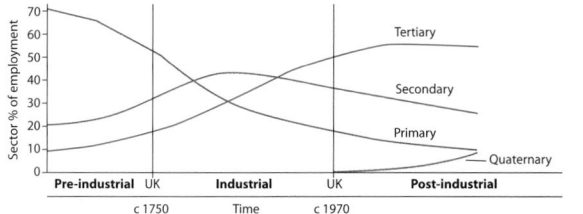

Figure 4.5 *Economic sector shifts in the UK*

Informal employment

The **informal sector** employs millions of people across the world, especially in LICs, but it is unofficial. People working in this sector don't pay tax on the money they earn, but equally the state can't protect informal workers from exploitation.

Causes

Rural–urban migration is the motor for the informal sector as people move from the countryside to towns to find work.

Characteristics

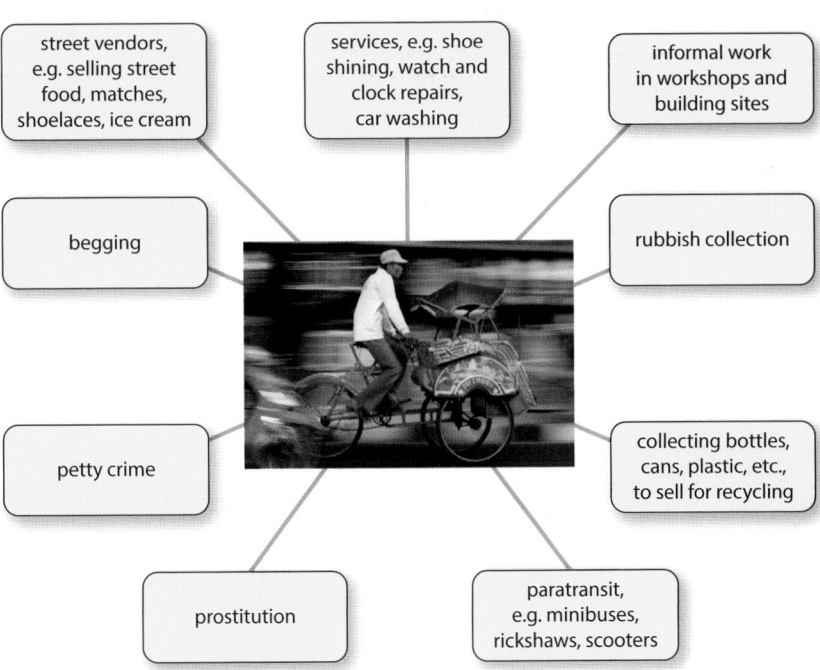

street vendors, e.g. selling street food, matches, shoelaces, ice cream

services, e.g. shoe shining, watch and clock repairs, car washing

informal work in workshops and building sites

begging

rubbish collection

petty crime

collecting bottles, cans, plastic, etc., to sell for recycling

prostitution

paratransit, e.g. minibuses, rickshaws, scooters

Figure 4.6a *Some characteristics of the informal sector*

People move to the city looking for jobs and better lifestyles

↓

Soon there are far more people than there are jobs

↓

High competition for jobs means employers can pay really low wages

↓

Then even people who have jobs still need to find other sources of income

↓

Growth occurs in the informal sector

Figure 4.6b *Rural–urban migration is the main cause for the growth of the informal sector*

Advantages and disadvantages

👍 Helps people make a living.

👍 Products and services are cheap enough for other poor people to afford.

👎 Children are often involved in the informal sector. They are then not educated and are often exploited.

👎 Working conditions are not regulated and can be very dangerous.

👎 No tax is paid, so the government and country have less money.

In a few countries the informal sector is estimated to be worth more than 50 per cent of GNP – that's huge! This includes relatively wealthy countries such as Nigeria and Thailand. By contrast, it is estimated to be worth just 9 per cent of the USA's GNP.

The growth and location of tertiary and quaternary activities

The tertiary sector can only fully develop when enough people have **disposable income** to spend on services.

Location factors

Primary sector and secondary sector activities often have strong **location** needs. For example, a steel mill needs supplies of raw material, energy supplies and access to markets.

Tertiary sector activities have fewer location requirements. **Accessibility** is most important: they need to be located where the maximum number of people can access their services.

- Shops, offices and entertainment services cluster in city CBDs because this is where all transport routes into the city meet. It is the most accessible part of the city.

- Out of town locations (on the urban fringe) are now becoming even better than the CBD:

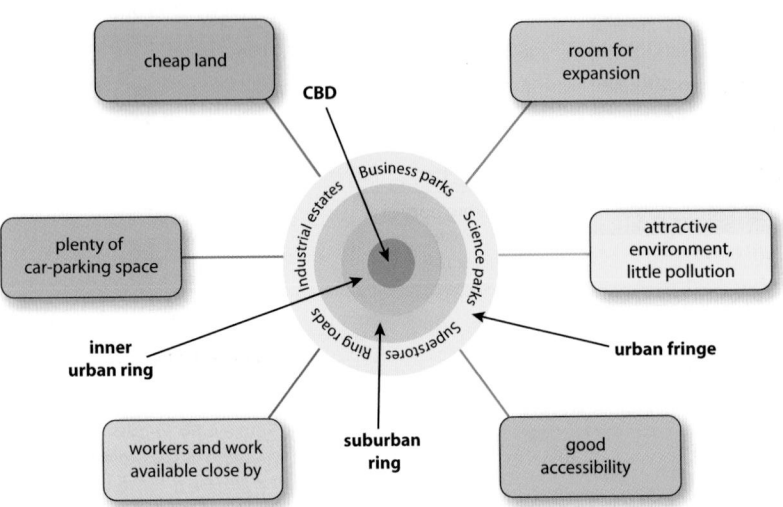

Figure 4.7 *The attractions of the urban fringe*

TOP TIP
Make sure you know a case study about the factors affecting the development and location of one hi-tech industry.

Footloose industries

Because of the internet and internet-based telephone services, many service industries can now be located anywhere and still make the same amount of money. Industries that can locate anywhere like this are called 'footloose' industries.

Many quaternary sector, **hi-tech industries** are footloose. Even so, quaternary sector activities are frequently found in a cluster because:

- universities often set up research and development science parks near their main campus

- government tries to encourage hi-tech companies to particular areas (to create jobs) by offering them incentives

- companies like to be near other companies working in the same field so that they can supply eachother and so that they can access a skilled workforce.

The changing location of manufacturing

There has been a gradual global shift in manufacturing from the HICs to the MICs – Brazil, Russia, India and China.

China is responsible for around 15 per cent of global manufacturing.

Why has this change happened?

Location factors are still important for many manufacturing industries, but some factors have been cancelled out by technological developments:

- **Transport** – container shipping has revolutionised transport. Products can be shipped from any country to big markets around the world quickly and cheaply.

- **Communications** – the internet means that a head office can communicate instantaneously with its manufacturers located anywhere in the world.

- **Energy** – access to energy is the same in almost all parts of the world, and energy costs can be much lower in LICs.

As soon as these important location factors became similar all over the world, other factors become important:

- **Labour costs** – labour (workers) is much cheaper in LICs and MICs than in HICs.

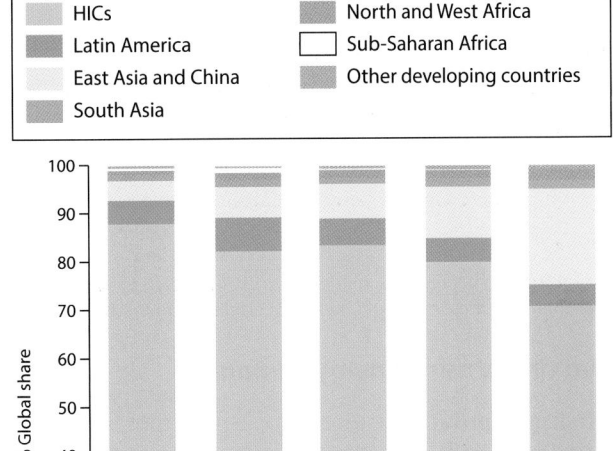

Key
- HICs
- Latin America
- East Asia and China
- South Asia
- North and West Africa
- Sub-Saharan Africa
- Other developing countries

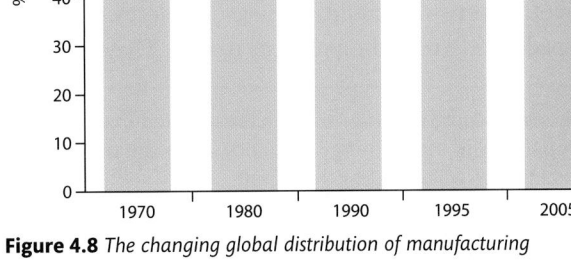

Figure 4.8 *The changing global distribution of manufacturing*

- **Government policy** – governments of MICs and LICs offer big incentives to companies to locate there, such as tax breaks and ready-made factories.

- **Transnational corporations (TNCs)** – global companies have emerged, with the capital (money) and scale to locate different parts of their operations in different countries. They manufacture where labour is cheap and locate their sales departments in big markets.

Deindustrialisation

As manufacturing has moved from HICs to MICs, the former industrial regions of HICs have been hit hard. In these regions, whole communities depended on heavy industry. When heavy industry declined, many people lost their jobs. This caused major social problems.

TOP TIP ✓
Make sure you know a case study of a deindustrialised area, the causes and consequences of deindustrialisation and any re-development of the area.

Rising energy demand and the energy gap

Rising demand for energy

Figure 4.9 shows that energy consumption (use) has grown rapidly in the last 40 years. Consumption has increased in all regions, but especially in China and the rest of Asia and South America.

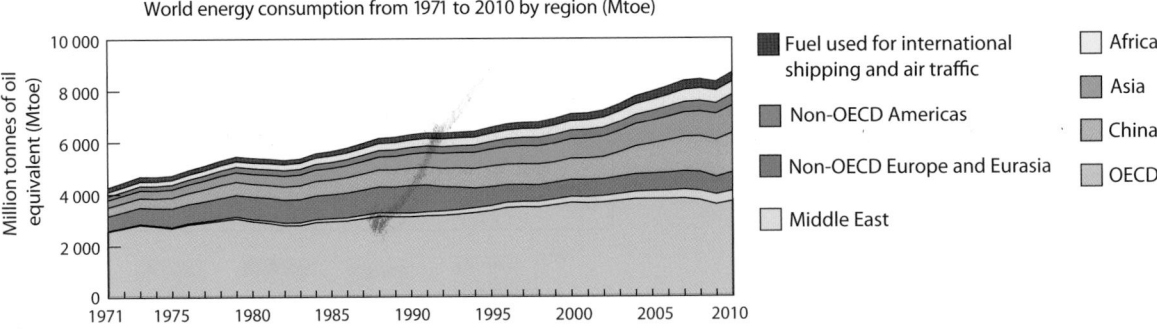

Figure 4.9 *World energy consumption from 1971 to 2010 by region. OECD countries are HICs, non-OECD countries in Europe are the former Communist countries and non-OECD countries in the Americas are South American countries (Source: IEA 2012)*

What drives rising energy demand?

- **Rising population** – more people need more energy.

- **Development** – as countries develop, energy use increases. People progress from riding bicycles to mopeds, and from riding mopeds to cars. They buy fridges, air conditioners and TVs.

> The energy company ExxonMobil has estimated that the world will be using 40 per cent more energy in 2040 compared with today. Energy efficiency will mean that HIC energy use will not change. MIC and LIC energy consumption will grow by 60 per cent.

The energy gap

- The **energy gap** is the difference between a country's demand for energy and its ability to produce that energy from its own energy sources.

- The top three oil-exporting countries in 2012 were Russia, Saudi Arabia and India. These countries have big energy surpluses.

- The top three oil importers in 2012 were Japan, China and Mexico. These countries have a big energy gap.

- Countries with energy gaps work hard to find ways to reduce them.

The need for energy efficiency

Make sure you know and understand these key terms:

- **Non-renewable energy:** energy sources that cannot be replaced once they are used up. For example, fossil fuels.

- **Renewable energy**: energy sources that can be used again and again. For example, solar power.

Finite energy

Non-renewable energy sources are finite – there will come a point when they will run out. Currently, oil is the most-used energy source. **Peak oil**, the point at which the production of oil will start to decline, is estimated to occur somewhere between 2015 and 2050.

The need for energy efficiency

As soon as finite supplies start to run out, prices for energy shoot up:

- this makes economic development much harder

- countries with an energy gap have to pay much more

- countries with an energy surplus grow very powerful, wars become more likely.

Non-renewable energy sources are closely linked to the enhanced greenhouse effect:

- if MICs and LICs fuel their economic development with non-renewable energy, global warming will be made much worse

- alternative sources of oil may be available, e.g. in the Arctic, but extracting oil from them could cause much environmental damage.

Currently, people in HICs are very wasteful of energy. Energy gaps could be significantly reduced if energy use was more efficient. If development in MICs and LICs was also energy efficient, the impacts of the energy crisis would be reduced considerably.

Ways to use energy more efficiently

Here are five ways. There are many more:

1. insulate buildings – heating them uses less energy

2. turn down heating and air conditioning

3. switch off appliances when they are not being used

4. use products for longer before replacing them – this reduces the energy used in making and disposing of them

5. use public transport, walk or cycle for short trips instead of going by car.

PRACTICAL SKILLS
Research the main sources for the energy used in your country.

Renewable versus non-renewable sources of energy

Different types of non-renewable and renewable energy have their own advantages and disadvantages. The following fact files give you the information you need for:

- non-renewable sources: coal, oil and natural gas
- both non-renewable and renewable: fuel wood and nuclear energy
- renewable sources: HEP, geothermal, wind, tidal, solar and biofuel.

Fact file: Coal

Status – non-renewable fossil fuel

Description – formed underground from decaying plant and animal matter

Lifespan – over 200 years

% share of world energy use – 23

Main producers – USA, China, Australia, India, South Africa, Russian Federation

Energy uses – electricity, heating, coke

✔ **advantages** – high world reserves; newer mines are highly mechanised

✘ **disadvantages** – pollution CO_2, the major greenhouse gas responsible for global warming; SO_2, the main gas responsible for acid rain; mining can be difficult and dangerous; opencast pits destroy land; heavy/bulky to transport

Fact file: Oil

Status – non-renewable fossil fuel

Description – formed underground from decaying animal and plant matter

Lifespan – about 50 years

% share of world energy use – about 37

Main producers – Saudi Arabia, USA, Russian Federation, Iran, Mexico, Venezuela, China

Energy uses – electricity, petroleum, diesel, fuel oils, liquid petroleum gas, coke and many non-energy uses, e.g. plastics, medicines, fertilisers

✔ **advantages** – variety of uses; fairly easy to transport; efficient; less pollution than coal

✘ **disadvantages** – low reserves; some air pollution; danger of spills (especially at sea) and explosions

Fact file: Natural gas

Status – non-renewable fossil fuel

Description – formed underground from decaying animal and plant matter; often found with oil

Lifespan – 60 years

% share of world energy – 23

Main producers – Russian Federation, USA, Canada, UK, Algeria

Energy uses – electricity, cooking, heating

✔ **advantages** – efficient; clean – least polluting of the fossil fuels; easy to transport

✘ **disadvantages** – explosions; some air pollution

Fact file: Fuel wood

Status – non-renewable/renewable

Description – trees, usually in natural environment, but can be grown specifically for fuel

Lifespan – variable within each country, but declining except where there is large-scale reafforestation

% share of world energy use – about 10

Main producers of energy – LICs, especially in Africa and Asia

Energy uses – heating, cooking (also used for building homes and fences)

✔ **advantages** – easily available, collected daily by local people; free; replanting possible

✘ **disadvantages** – trees used up quickly; time-consuming – wood must be collected daily; deforestation leads to other problems (soil erosion, desertification); replanting cannot keep pace with consumption

Fact file: Nuclear energy

Status – classified by some as non-renewable because of reliance on uranium as a fuel; others regard it as renewable in that the nuclear fuel may be re-used

Description – heavy metal (uranium) element found naturally in rock deposits

Lifespan – unknown

% share of world energy consumption – 6

Main producers of energy – USA, France, Japan, Germany, Russian Federation

Energy uses – used in a chain reaction to produce heat for electricity

✔ **advantages** – clean; fewer greenhouse gases; efficient, uses very small amounts of raw materials; small amounts of waste

✘ **disadvantages** – dangers of radiation; high cost of building and decommissioning power stations; problems over disposal of waste; nuclear accidents like Chernobyl raised public fears

Fact file: Hydroelectric power

Status – renewable

Description – good, regular supply of water needed; water held in a reservoir, channelled through pipes to a turbine

% share of world energy use – 3

Main producers – Canada, USA, Brazil, China, Russian Federation

Energy uses – electricity

✔ **advantages** – very clean; reservoirs/dams can also control flooding/provide water in times of shortage; often in remote, mountainous, sparsely populated areas

✘ **disadvantages** – large areas of land flooded; silt trapped behind dam; lake silts up; visual pollution from pylons and dam

Fact file: Geothermal

Status – renewable

Description – boreholes can be drilled below ground to use the Earth's natural heat; cold water is pumped down, hot water or steam channelled back

% share of world energy consumption – < 1

Main producers – Japan, New Zealand, Russian Federation, Iceland, Hungary

Energy uses – electricity, direct heating

✔ **advantages** – many potential sites, but most are in volcanic areas at the moment

✘ **disadvantages** – sulphuric gases; expensive to develop; very high temperature can create maintenance problems

Fact file: Wind

Status – renewable

Description – wind drives blades to turn turbines

% share of world energy – < 1

Main producers – Denmark, California USA

Energy uses – electricity

✔ **advantages** – very clean; no air pollution; small-scale and large-scale schemes possible; cheap to run

✘ **disadvantages** – winds are unpredictable and not constant; visual and noise pollution in quiet, rural areas; many turbines needed to produce sufficient energy.

Fact file: Tidal

Status – renewable

Description – tidal water drives turbines

% share of world energy consumption – insignificant

Main producers – France, Russian Federation

Energy uses – electricity

✔ **advantages** – large schemes could produce a lot of electricity; clean; barrage can protect coasts from erosion

✘ **disadvantages** – very expensive to build; few suitable sites; disrupts coastal ecosystems and shipping.

Fact file: Solar

Status – renewable

Description – solar panels or photovoltaic cells using sunlight

% share of world energy – < 1

Main producers – USA, India

Energy uses – direct heating, electricity

✔ **advantages** – could be used in most parts of the world; unlimited supplies; clean; can be built into new buildings; efficient

✘ **disadvantages** – expensive; needs sunlight, cloud/night means solar energy is reduced; large amounts of energy require technological development and reduction in costs of PVs (photovoltaic cells)

Fact file: Biofuel

Status – renewable

Description – fermented animal or plant waste or crops (e.g. sugar cane); refuse incineration

% share of world energy consumption – < 1

Main producers – Argentina, Brazil, Japan, Germany, Denmark, India

Energy uses – ethanol, methane, electricity, heating

✔ **advantages** – widely available, especially in LICs; uses waste products; can be used at a local level

✘ **disadvantages** – can be expensive to set up; waste cannot be recycled; some pollution.

FIELDWORK INVESTIGATION
You may have investigated people's conflicting views on the use and impacts of renewable and non-renewable energy in your fieldwork.

1   Give an example of an economic activity from the
    primary sector.   *(1)*

2   What is meant by the abbreviation MIC?   *(1)*

3   Name **one** way that the importance of an
    economic sector to its total economy is
    measured.   *(1)*

4   What is meant by the term 'energy gap'?   *(2)*

5   What is the meaning of the term 'sectoral shift'? *(2)*

6   Study **Figure 4.10** which shows the economic
    sectors of Ethiopia, China and the UK.

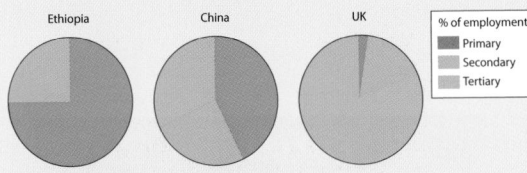

Figure 4.10 *Number of people employed in each sector for a typical LIC, MIC and HIC*

   a) Describe what **Figure 4.10** shows about
       Ethiopia's economy.   *(2)*

   b) Explain why a dominant tertiary sector is
       only found in HICs.   *(2)*

   c) What changes to the relative importance of
       each of the three economic sectors would
       you expect to see in China as that country
       develops?   *(4)*

7   What is meant by the term 'footloose'?   *(2)*

8   Describe how the tertiary sector develops.   *(4)*

9   Give **two** reasons for the shift in manufacturing
    from HICs to MICs.   *(4)*

10 Outline **two** reasons for the rising demand for
    energy in MICs and LICs.   *(4)*

11 Describe the factors affecting the location of a
    named hi-tech industry.   *(6)*

12 Explain the advantages and disadvantages of
    non-renewable sources of energy.   *(6)*

13 Using a case study, describe the causes and
    consequences of deindustrialisation.   *(9)*

Exam Section C question

14 How could newspaper articles and blogs be used
    to collect local reactions to a renewable energy
    development, such as the siting of a new
    windfarm?   *(4)*

Chapter 5: Ecosystems and rural environments

Biomes

Make sure you know and understand these key terms:

- **Ecosystem**: an organic community of plants and animals interacting with their environment.

- **Biome**: an ecosystem at the world scale; usually defined by its dominant vegetation type, e.g. tropical rainforest.

> There are eleven biomes altogether and their distribution is controlled by climate, especially temperature and moisture.

Tundra: bitterly cold, dark winters, low precipitation → grasses, mosses and lichens, occasional stunted/dwarf trees.	**Coniferous forest:** cold winters and cool summers → needle-like leaves on trees to withstand the cold and reduce moisture loss.	**Deciduous forest:** low winter temperatures → trees shed leaves in the winter.	**Mediterranean:** summer drought and winter rain → plants adapted to cope with drought, e.g. small trees, low scrub, grassland.	**Temperate grassland:** climate unsuitable for trees and shrubs → grasses dominate.

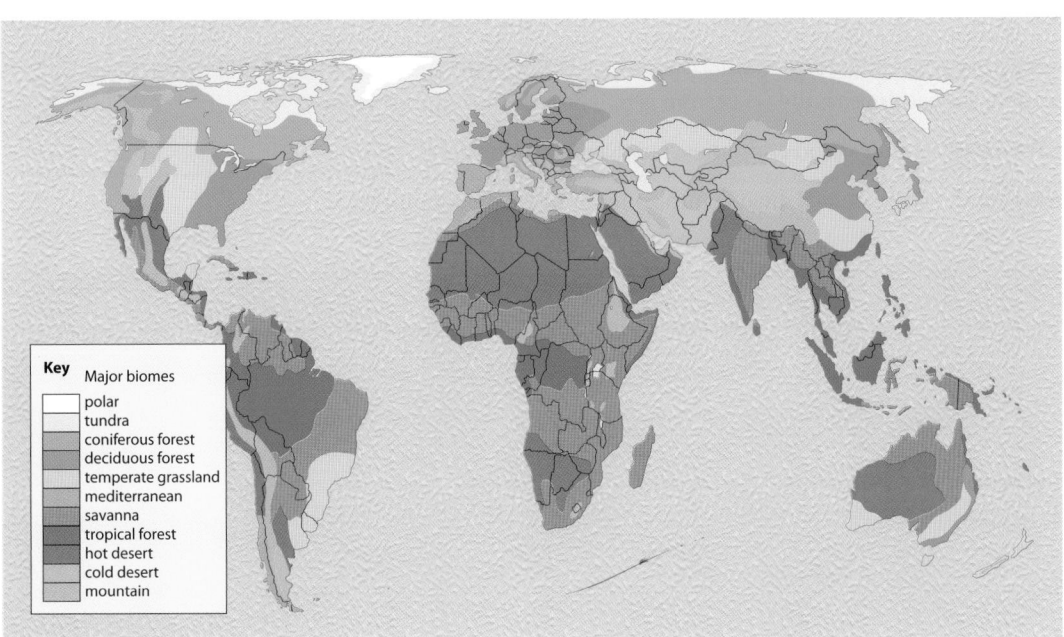

Figure 5.1 *Biomes of the world*

Savanna: close to Equator means warm temperatures, but also dry → scattered bushes and grasses.	**Mountain:** temperature drops with altitude → mountain biomes are similar to tundra.	**Tropical rainforest:** close to Equator, but both warm and wet → optimal conditions for plant growth and most productive biome on Earth.	**Desert:** lack of rainfall, can be hot if in tropics, or cold if outside tropics → general lack of vegetation.

Ecosystems and their components

Ecosystems consist of organisms (plants and animals) and their physical environment (sunlight, air, water, rock and soil). The living organisms and their physical environment are closely linked together in a delicate balance.

Ecosystems have three main components: inputs, stores and outputs.

- **Inputs** include energy from the Sun, rainfall, nutrients from the soil and minerals weathered from rocks.

- **Stores** are the plants, the animals and the soil in the ecosystem. Inputs are cycled around these stores.

- **Outputs** from the ecosystem include eroded soil, water and carbon dioxide.

Adaptation and succession

Ecosystems develop over time. **Figure 5.2**, the cross-section of a coastal sand dune, illustrates some key ecosystem processes:

- **Adaptation:** the newest dunes start close to the shore. The conditions are difficult: salty and very poor, unstable, fast-draining soil. The plants that colonise these dunes are specially adapted to the conditions.

- **Succession:** over time, soil conditions improve. Other plant species are able to take over. Eventually no more new species appear; the ecosystem is in balance: the 'climax' stage.

- **Biodiversity:** as succession continues, biodiversity increases.

- **Zonation:** the ecosystem is divided into zones of different conditions.

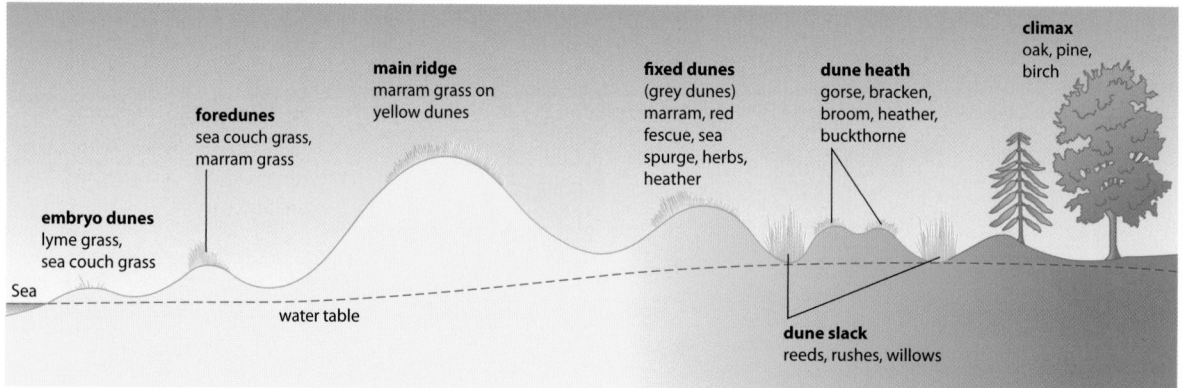

Figure 5.2 *Coastal sand dune ecosystem*

The temperate grassland biome

> **Temperate grasslands** are a biome dominated by grasses and rich soils. They are found in the mid-latitude interiors of continents: the prairies of North America, the steppes of Asia and the pampas of South America.

Vegetation grows slowly because of the cold winters, which means a limited food supply for animals. But the soils of this biome are very rich: as the grasses die in winter they release minerals into the soil.

In an ecosystem, a **food web** shows what is eating what, and therefore how energy moves from plants to animals.

PRACTICAL SKILLS

The rich, black soils of the temperate grasslands are called chernozems, from the Russian чернозём: 'black earth'. Do you know how to produce an annotated sketch from a chernozem soil profile photo?

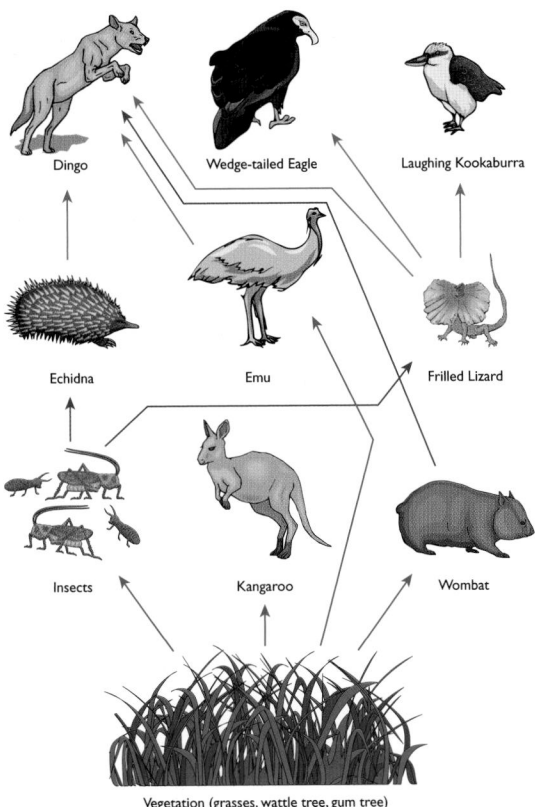

Figure 5.3 *A food web for the Australian grasslands*

TOP TIP

Make sure you know a case study of an ecosystem that you can use to explain ecological processes.

Goods and services

> **Goods** are material things or products that can be taken directly from an ecosystem and put to use (e.g. timber from a forest). **Services** are long-term benefits that people can gain from ecosystems (e.g. forests trap carbon dioxide from the atmosphere).

Temperate grasslands can become very valuable agricultural regions because of their rich soils. However, soil nutrients have to be replaced once the grass cover has been removed and the soil must be protected from erosion by the wind and rain.

When European settlers took control of the Great Plains of the US Midwest, first they hunted bison to near extinction, then they ploughed up the grasslands and failed to protect the soil from loss of fertility and from erosion. By the 1930s the soil was ruined and blew away, creating the 'Dust Bowl'.

Characteristics of rural environments

> **Rural** environments (the countryside or non-urbanised areas) often have small settlements, low population density and open space used for farming.

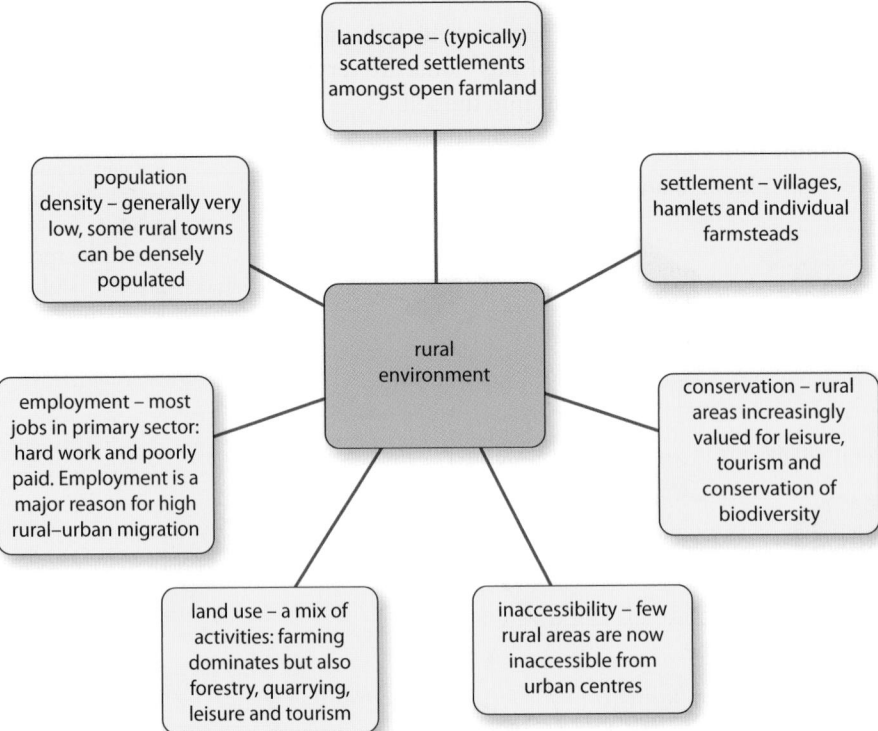

landscape – (typically) scattered settlements amongst open farmland

population density – generally very low, some rural towns can be densely populated

settlement – villages, hamlets and individual farmsteads

rural environment

employment – most jobs in primary sector: hard work and poorly paid. Employment is a major reason for high rural–urban migration

conservation – rural areas increasingly valued for leisure, tourism and conservation of biodiversity

land use – a mix of activities: farming dominates but also forestry, quarrying, leisure and tourism

inaccessibility – few rural areas are now inaccessible from urban centres

Figure 5.4 *The characteristics of rural environments*

The Lake District National Park

> The Lake District is a mainly rural region in the UK. It was made a national park in 1951.

TOP TIP ✔

Make sure you know a case study of a national park or protected area – how it is managed and the reasons it is protected.

Promote tourism: advertise beautiful scenery

Promote tourism: market wide range of activities – walking, climbing, rock-climbing, birdwatching, sightseeing, mountain biking

Protect traditional farming, protect wildlife

Welcome to
BUTTERMERE
Please drive carefully

Manage tourist traffic, ease congestion

Maintain footpaths, repair erosion

Figure 5.5 *The Lake District National Park: protection and management*

The farm as a system

In the farm system, higher **outputs** can be achieved when changes are made to some **inputs**. For example, in a dry climate, irrigation increases the water inputs. In a cool climate, glasshouses increase the temperature inputs.

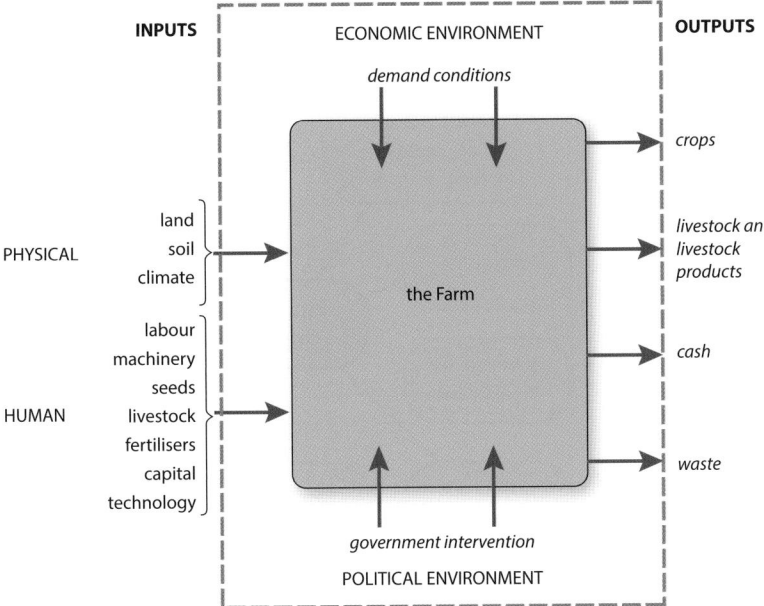

Figure 5.6 *The farm as a system*

Different types of farming

- **Subsistence farming** is where the farm feeds the farming family. **Commercial farming** is where everything is grown to be sold.

- **Arable farming** means growing crops. **Pastoral farming** means rearing animals. **Mixed farming** is a little of both.

- **Extensive farming** is large areas of land producing relatively low yield. **Intensive farming** is a small area of land producing a high yield.

> **FIELDWORK INVESTIGATION**
> You may have explored how a farm works as a system as part of your fieldwork investigation. Can you relate what you found to this diagram?

> There are many different ways of increasing agricultural production: irrigation and **GM** crops are just two examples.

> **TOP TIP**
> Make sure you know a case study about two ways of raising agricultural production.

Irrigation in Bangladesh

Population growth has increased the demand for food. There is a long dry season between October and April. **Irrigation** (from wells) means rice can be grown all year round.

Challenges:

- Too much irrigation leads to waterlogged crops.

- Water evaporation leads to salinisation, which poisons crops.

- Over-extraction means wells have to be dug deeper and deeper.

GM crops

Genetic modification of crops gives them special qualities, e.g. resistance to disease. The USA has a relatively long history of commercial GM farming, starting in 1994 with the Flavr Savr tomato that was resistant to rotting.

Challenges:

- Resistance in many countries (e.g. EU) to GM: 'Frankenstein foods'.

- Fears that GM varieties will contaminate other crops.

Food shortages in LICs

When droughts hit grain production in the Midwest of the USA, for example, HICs sourced grain from elsewhere, albeit at higher prices. But LICs cannot always afford to tackle food shortages this way, sometimes with terrible consequences.

TOP TIP
Older textbooks and resources may cover food overproduction in HICs. This is no longer required for the International GCSE course.

Causes

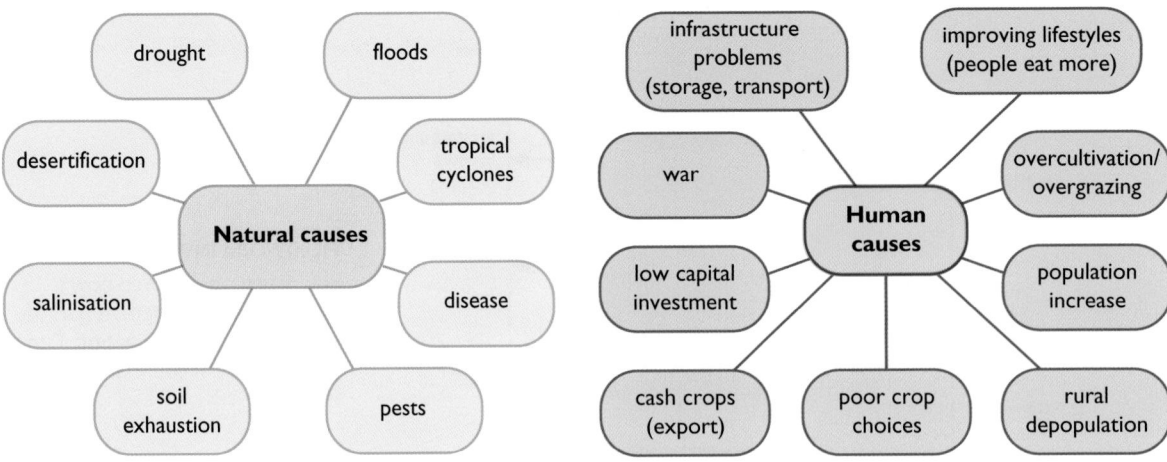

Figure 5.7 *Natural causes of food shortages in LICs*

Figure 5.8 *Human causes of food shortages in LICs*

Consequences

Food shortages in LICs can mean:

- poor people in LICs suffer malnutrition, which makes them weak and unable to work

- food prices rise, increasing poverty, which encourages rural debt; also rural–urban migration

- marginal land brought into cultivation, increasing risk of environmental degradation.

The Green Revolution

This was an attempt in the 20th century to tackle food shortages in LICs by:

- developing **HYVs** – high-yielding varieties of grain crops

- increasing use of irrigation

- developing synthetic pesticides and herbicides

- modernising farm techniques.

The attempt worked – to an extent: grain production doubled in many LICs, but African countries often did not benefit as much as others. Other problems:

- reliance on chemical fertilisers and pesticides: expensive and polluting

- reduction in the variety of crops grown: monocultures

- forced many farmers into debt to pay for inputs.

Rural changes in LICs

Changes in LIC rural areas are linked to three main processes – population growth, rural–urban migration and economic development.

Rural depopulation is often associated with **rural–urban migration**. This means there are fewer farmers, so less food is grown. Worse than this, it is usually the young men who leave for the city, leaving old men behind to farm the land.

Population growth happens fastest in cities, putting increased strain on rural regions to supply food and fuel. As more and more people leave for cities, rural regions become more and more impoverished.

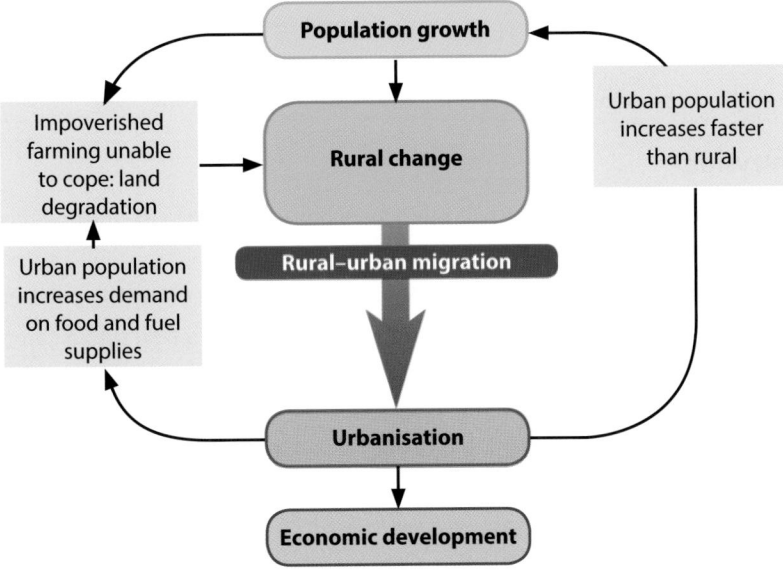

Figure 5.9 *Causes of rural change in LICs*

Cash crops

In some LICs **cash crops** are grown for export to HICs. Examples of this include coffee, tea, cocoa and fresh flowers.

- This type of farming replaces farming that grows food, exacerbating food shortages.

- It is often large agribusinesses that run farms rather than local farmers.

- High use of fertilisers and pesticides can cause environmental problems.

Poverty is deeply rooted in rural areas in LICs. For example, more than half of Kenya's 31 million people are poor and around 75 per cent of these live in rural areas.

Rural changes in HICs

Rural settlement changes in HICs depend on how accessible the rural area is from urban centres. Remote rural areas face different pressures from rural areas closer to cities.

Commuter belt

In many HICs city workers decide that the benefits of rural living outweigh the challenges of commuting to work everyday, and they move to commuter belt locations. These rural villages and towns are then changed by the new residents:

- dormitory character – new residents only come home to sleep; they shop and use services in the city during the working day, not where they live
- price increases – city workers have higher wages than rural residents and push up the price of village properties
- new estates are built on the edge of the old villages.

Accessible countryside

These rural areas are outside the commuter belt but accessible as a day trip from urban centres. Here, changes come from new economic activities.

- Farming is important in these areas but mechanisation means it does not employ many people.
- Some farms diversify to provide more sources of income, e.g. turning a field into a campsite, opening a farm shop, etc.
- Leisure and tourism activities are popular, e.g. pony trekking, sightseeing, historic tours, etc.
- Retirement migration – as people are living longer, more are choosing to retire to rural locations.

Remote countryside

The two most significant changes here are **depopulation** and the decline of farming.

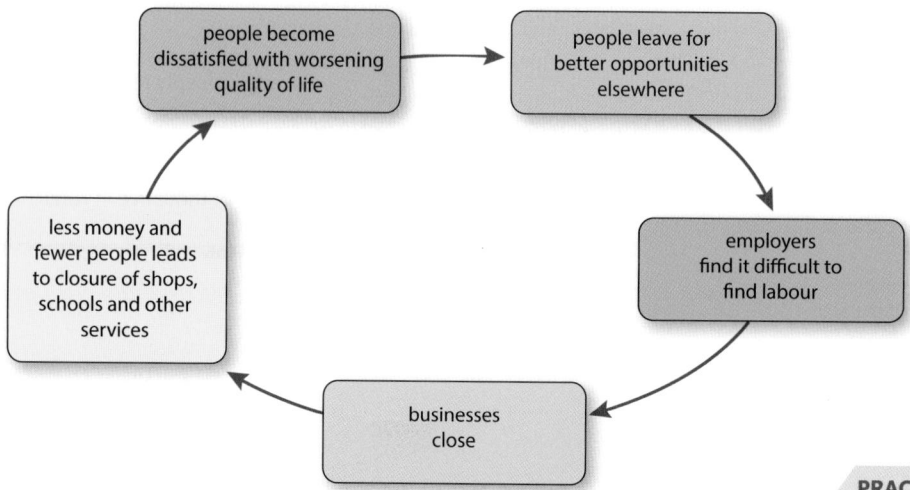

Figure 5.10 *Depopulation and decline*

However, in some remote rural areas this downwards spiral is being checked by **counterurbanisation**. This is when people who are dissatisfied with urban life leave for other locations.

PRACTICAL SKILLS

Do you know how to identify and evaluate the location of rural settlements based on map evidence/photo evidence?

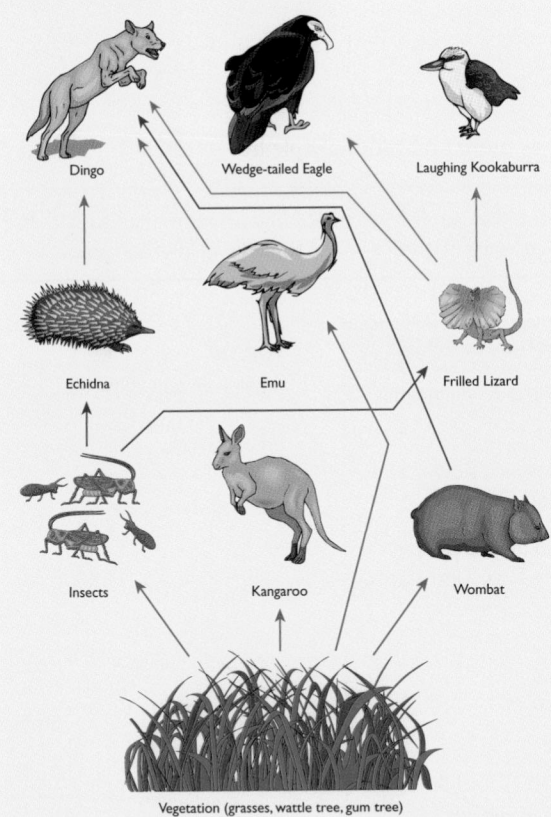

Dingo

Wedge-tailed Eagle

Laughing Kookaburra

Echidna

Emu

Frilled Lizard

Insects

Kangaroo

Wombat

Vegetation (grasses, wattle tree, gum tree)

Figure 5.11

1 Study **Figure 5.11** which shows a food web from an Australian ecosystem. What biome does this ecosystem belong to? *(1)*

2 Give an example of an organism shown in **Figure 5.11** that corresponds to each of the following levels of the ecosystem. The first one is completed for you:

Level 1: Producers (plants) ***grasses***

Level 2: Primary consumers (herbivores)

Level 3: Secondary consumers (carnivores and omnivores)

Level 4: Tertiary consumers (top predators) *(3)*

3 Define the term 'intensive agriculture'. *(2)*

4 What is suburbanisation? *(2)*

5 Name **two** types of farming. *(2)*

6 Describe **two** ways in which the Green Revolution aimed to improve agriculture in LICs. *(4)*

7 Explain **two** ways in which outputs from the farming system can be increased. *(2)*

8 Describe **two** examples of intensive agriculture, one that is characteristic of LICs and one that is characteristic of HICs. *(4)*

9 Explain what is meant by the goods and services of an ecosystem. Examples may help your answer. *(6)*

10 Explain the causes and consequences of rural–urban migration for rural areas in LICs. *(6)*

11 Explain the arguments for and against genetically modified crops. *(6)*

12 Explain the causes and consequences of food shortages in LICs. *(6)*

13 Discuss the advantages and disadvantages of irrigation as a way of increasing the outputs from farming in one named LIC. *(9)*

Exam Section C question

14 Identify **two** possible risks associated with a transect survey across a sand dune ecosystem. *(4)*

People and their environments (Section B)

Chapter 6: Urban environments

The nature of urbanisation

Make sure you know and understand this key term:

- **Urbanisation**: the process of becoming more urban, as more and more people live in towns and cities.

> Between 1950 and 2000, the world's population more than doubled but the urban population more than tripled. In 2007 population experts announced that, for the first time ever, over 50 per cent of people lived in urban areas.

Rapid urbanisation rates in LICs...	Slower urbanization rates in HICs...
High rates of rural–urban migration	Large proportion of the population is already urban
Natural increase is greatest in cities	Economic development is slower and not all is urban-based
Most new economic developments are in cities	Counterurbanisation means people are swapping city life for country living

TOP TIP

Make sure you know the factors affecting the rate of urbanisation.

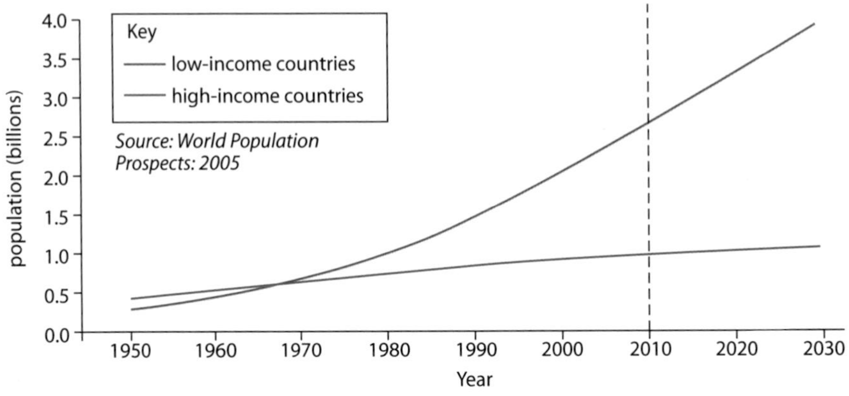

Figure 6.1 Urbanisation in HICs and LICs

As the city grows, **suburbanisation** pushes it outwards:

- transport improvements mean people can live further out but still travel into the city centre for work

- building developments follow the new transport routes: new, lower-density housing promises improved living conditions

- overcrowding, congestion and rising prices in the older parts of the city cause declining quality of living conditions.

Could you map the changing global distribution of megacities?

Megacities

> **Megacities** have a population of more than 10 million. In 2011 there were officially 21 megacities and there are likely to be 30 by 2015. Most are in Asia.

Factors driving the growth of megacities:

- rapid economic growth

- rapid population growth

- economies of scale – everything needed by businesses is close together

- multiplier effect – more jobs means more people come to the city, which makes more jobs possible, which attracts more people to the city, etc.

The problems of rapid urbanisation

Rapid and unplanned urbanisation creates a range of problems, including congestion, transport, employment, crime and environmental quality.

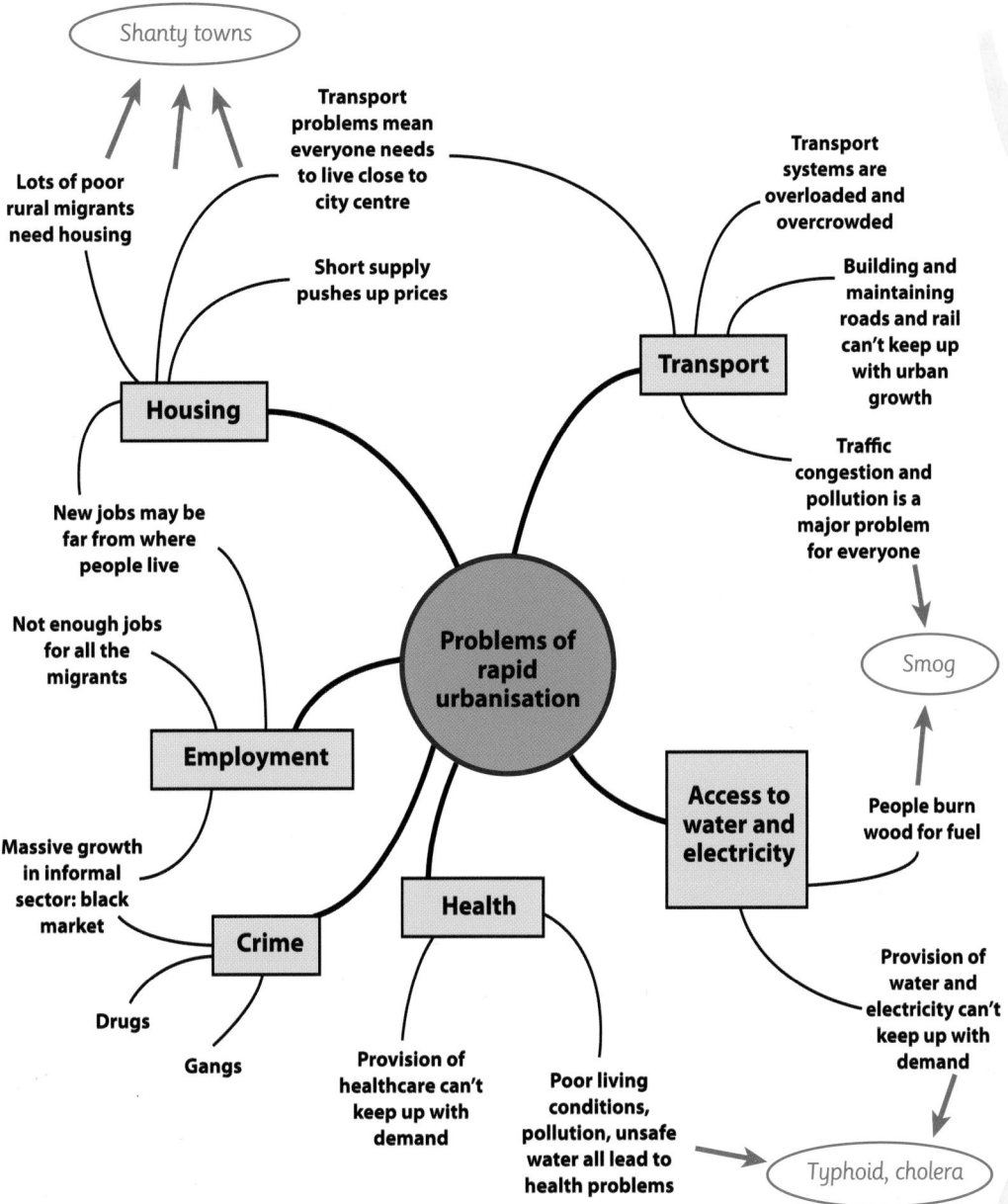

Figure 6.2 *Problems of rapid urbanisation*

Urban land use

Land is not worth the same in all areas of the city. It generally declines in value the further it is from the centre, although there are also peaks in land values along main transport routes.

- The CBD is near the centre of the city. This is the most accessible area. Retail businesses will pay high rents to be here because it is where the customers are.

- Manufacturing does not need to pay high CBD land prices for its prime location – manufacturing needs transport routes, room to expand and access to a labour force.

- As land gets cheaper towards the edge of the city it becomes affordable to build housing.

Because it also makes sense for companies doing the same thing to cluster together, cities become **segregated** by land use.

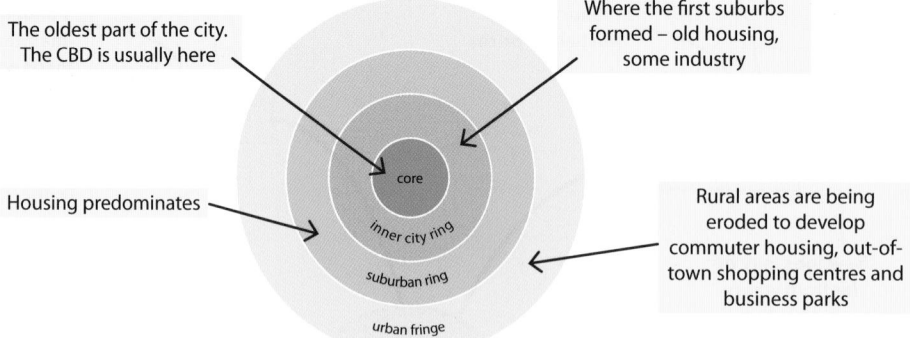

The oldest part of the city. The CBD is usually here

Where the first suburbs formed – old housing, some industry

Housing predominates

core

inner city ring

suburban ring

urban fringe

Rural areas are being eroded to develop commuter housing, out-of-town shopping centres and business parks

Figure 6.3 *The four zones of a city*

Segregation of people in cities

> Because land has different values in different areas across the city, people also become grouped into different locations according to their socio-economic status.

Social segregation

The richest people can afford to live anywhere in the city. The poorest can only afford to live where rents are cheapest and from where they can afford to get to work. In HICs this is often the **inner city** ring. Here, buildings are subdivided into many small flats. Population densities are very high.

Ethnic segregation

A ghetto is an area where one ethnic group forms the dominant population. Ghettos are often associated with immigration. Ghettos form because of external pressures on new immigrants, such as discrimination, but also as a result of internal factors, such as mutual support.

Case study: Zomba, a city in Malawi

TOP TIP ✓

Make sure you know a case study of one city, showing the land use patterns and the distribution of social/ethnic groups. You may have studied a different case study from the one outlined here. Make sure you revise the one you learned at school.

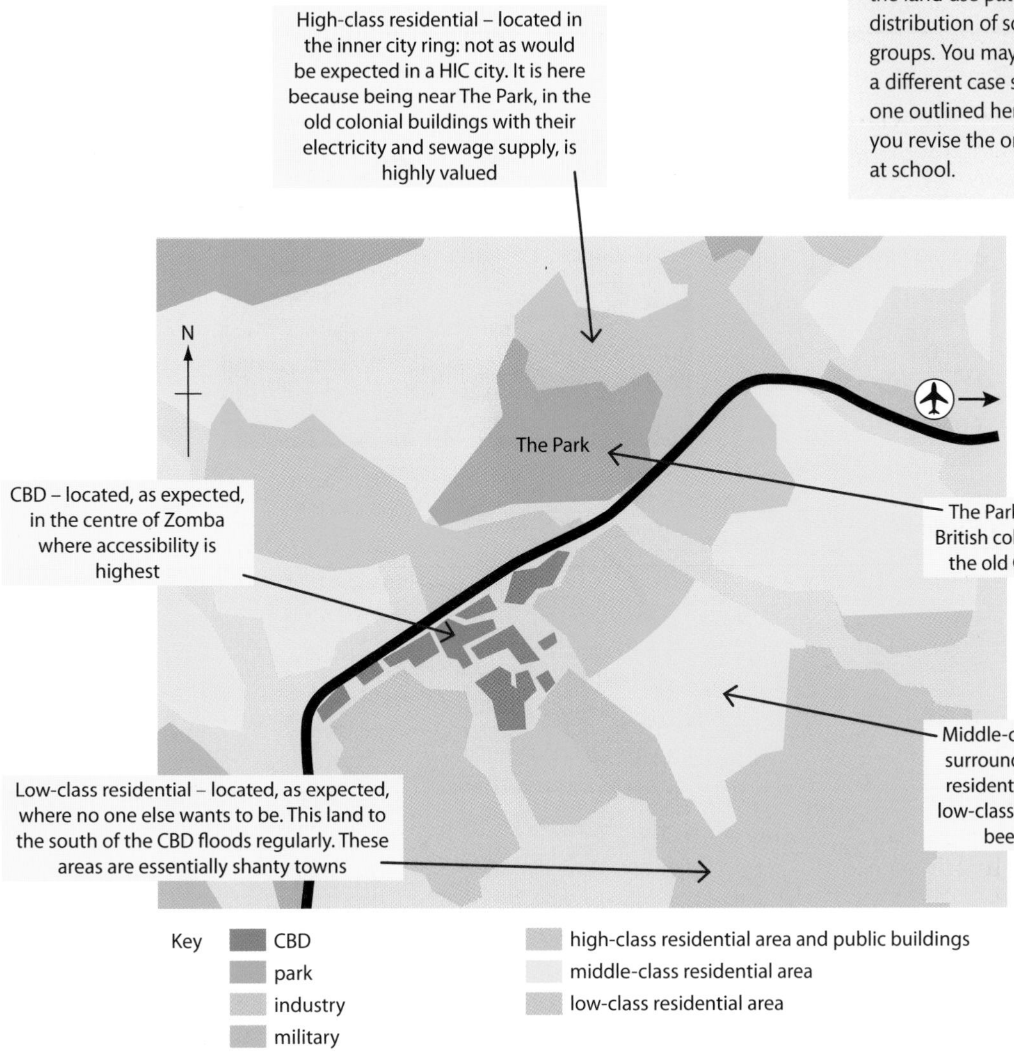

High-class residential – located in the inner city ring: not as would be expected in a HIC city. It is here because being near The Park, in the old colonial buildings with their electricity and sewage supply, is highly valued

The Park

The Park – a remnant of British colonial rule; part of the old Gymkhana Club

CBD – located, as expected, in the centre of Zomba where accessibility is highest

Middle-class residential – surrounds the high-class residential: this is former low-class housing that has been upgraded

Low-class residential – located, as expected, where no one else wants to be. This land to the south of the CBD floods regularly. These areas are essentially shanty towns

Key
- CBD
- park
- industry
- military
- high-class residential area and public buildings
- middle-class residential area
- low-class residential area

Figure 6.4 *The urban pattern of Zomba*

People and their environments (Section B)

FIELDWORK INVESTIGATION
You may have studied urban land use changes in your fieldwork. That work could also make an excellent case study.

Shanty towns: São Paulo's favelas

Shanty towns (also called squatter settlements) develop as a consequence of the rapid growth of urban areas in LICs.

TOP TIP ✓

Make sure you know a case study that contrasts a managed shanty town with an unmanaged one in a LIC. You may have studied a different case study from the one outlined here. Make sure you revise the one(s) you did at school.

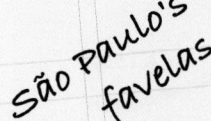

São Paulo's favelas

Location: Brazil's largest city. There are approximately 2500 favelas in São Paulo. Many have grown up around new factories, along main roads and railway lines, and in places that are near water (and often flood): river banks, gullies, floodplains.

Growth: for 40 years poor rural migrants have been setting up makeshift homes in the favelas. At first, the favelas were restricted to the outskirts. Now they have spread to all unoccupied parts of the city, including next to the CBD. Two million people now live in favelas – 20 per cent of São Paulo's population.

Problems: like all shanty towns, São Paulo's favelas are often built on unsafe land and, at first, they have no services: no electricity or piped water (for drinking and sanitation), no rubbish collection, no proper roads. Gang crime is often high. Rats and cockroaches are a real problem.

Self help: community groups in many of the favelas have campaigned to persuade the government to improve services, reduce crime and give favela children more of a future. Micro-loans have given small grants to local groups in some favelas to set up businesses.

Improvements: some of the older favelas now have basic infrastructure, brick buildings, services and shops. Some people are concerned that these improvements will now encourage more rural migrants to come to the city.

Urban change in HICs 1

Changes at the edges of HIC cities

> Changes occur in cities as they get older and as the needs of their inhabitants change. Changes are most obvious at the edge of the city: the **rural–urban fringe**.

Push and pull factors on the urban fringe

Here are three push factors that encourage people to move out from inside the city:

- housing is too cramped, old and expensive
- businesses cannot afford the space to expand
- pollution, congestion, social problems (crime).

And here are three pull factors, attracting people to the rural–urban fringe:

- land is cheaper so new houses can be bigger
- plenty of space for business to expand
- roads are less busy, air is fresher, social problems less obvious.

Figure 6.5 *Out-of-town retail parks need lots of space for parking, good transport links and a pleasant environment*

Housing, out-of-town retail parks, industrial estates and business parks spearhead the development of the rural–urban fringe:

- people want more spacious housing
- people want a more pleasant shopping experience: plenty of parking and a wide range of shops under one roof
- businesses want space to expand, lower rates and the chance to cluster with suppliers and research and development specialists.

Excellent communication routes are essential: commuting routes for housing developments, fast roads to bring in shoppers from all over the region for out-of-town retail parks and to transport materials and products for business parks and industrial estates.

Urban change in HICs 2

The greenfield versus brownfield debate

> Not everyone is happy about the loss of countryside to urban development. Environmentalists and others believe new developments should be built on **brownfield sites** inside the city, not **greenfield sites** outside the city.

Some HIC cities are surrounded by a green belt. A green belt restricts development to protect the countryside from urban sprawl. However, developers have often leap-frogged the green belt and developed the area beyond it instead.

Advantages and disadvantages of greenfield versus brownfield sites

Site	Advantages	Disadvantages
Brownfield	• Conserves countryside • Revives old urban areas • Services are already connected – gas, sewers, etc.	• Often expensive to clear the site • Might be surrounded by rundown areas • May be a long way from fast modern roads
Greenfield	• Cheaper and faster to build on • Clean slate: can plan efficient and attractive developments • Healthier environment	• Wildlife habitats are lost • Valuable farmland may be lost • Encourages urban sprawl

Southampton's rural–urban fringe: case study

Southampton has excellent motorway links, with the M3, M27 and M271. It also has a thriving port. However, a green belt restricts the expansion of city. A few developments have been allowed on greenfield land within the green belt to take advantage of the excellent transport links:

- Nursling Industrial Park – beside the M271: distribution and storage services

- Southampton Science Park – near the M3: hi-tech industries that benefit from access to R&D at Southampton University

- Hedge End Retail Park – close to the M27: one of the largest retail parks in the south of England

- Adanac Business Park – next to M271: modern business facilities, landscaped grounds.

TOP TIP

Make sure you know a case study of an HIC urban area and can explain how and why changes are taking place. You may have studied a different city than the example given here: make sure you revise the case study you did at school.

PRACTICAL SKILLS

Study photos and maps that show how urban areas near you have changed. You could also practise drawing annotated sketches to show the changes you've identified.

Deprivation and poverty in HIC cities

Make sure you know and understand this key term:

- **Deprivation**: when people lack what the rest of society considers 'normal', such as good housing, reasonable incomes or access to healthcare.

The symptoms of deprivation and poverty in the city

- Poor housing (slums).
- Unattractive living environment (graffiti, litter, vandalism).
- Poor quality services (shops, parks, schools, etc.).
- Unemployment, poor educational achievement.
- Crime and anti-social behaviour.

The locations of deprivation and poverty in the city

- Where the value of land is lowest (outskirts of the city).
- Where housing is old and substandard, and in the high-rise apartment blocks constructed in the 1960s and 1970s (inner city).

Changing fortunes of the inner city

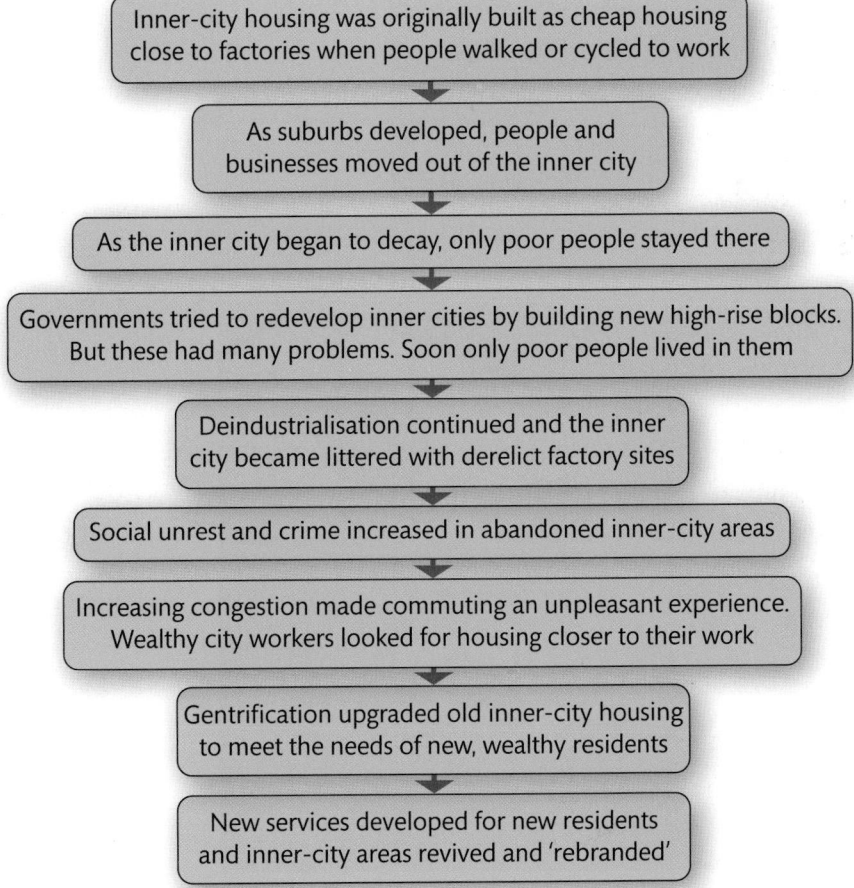

Figure 6.6 *The changing fortunes of inner-city areas*

Urban rebranding

Make sure you understand and can explain these key terms:

- **Urban regeneration**: the revival of old parts of the built-up area by either installing modern facilities in old buildings (known as renewal) or redevelopment (i.e. demolishing all existing buildings and starting afresh).

- **Rebranding**: regeneration that also tries to give an area a new image. Rebranded areas often have names and logos, e.g. MediaCityUK in Salford.

Local politicians and planners (urban managers) decide to improve an area

Establish that there are no obstacles or serious opposition to rebranding

Set up partnership between local government, developers and potential employers

Regeneration and/or rebranding work begins!

Figure 6.7 *The urban regeneration/ rebranding process*

Figure 6.8 *Redevelopment: this old industrial park was demolished to make way for the London Olympic site*

Figure 6.9 *Renewal: this old factory area in Toronto has been developed into a cultural centre*

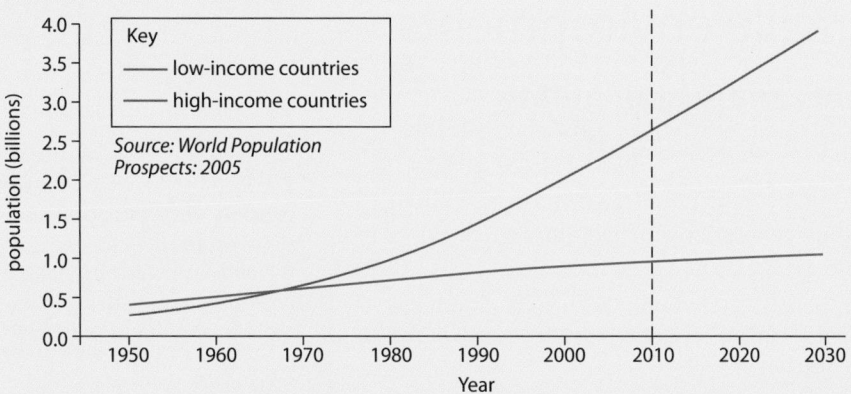

Figure 6.10

1 Study **Figure 6.10** above which shows the rate of urbanisation in HICs and LICs. How many people lived in LIC urban areas in 2010? *(1)*

2 Which of the following is the best definition of urbanisation?

a) The process of becoming more urban

b) The revival of older parts of the built-up environment

c) When a city reaches a population exceeding 10 million. *(1)*

3 Name an example of a shanty town. *(1)*

4 Give **one** example of a symptom of deprivation or poverty in a HIC city. *(1)*

5 Give **two** reasons for the high rates of urbanisation in LICs. *(2)*

6 Define the term 'suburbanisation'. *(2)*

7 Name **two** examples of megacities. *(2)*

8 Give **two** reasons why a retail park would choose an out-of-town location. *(2)*

9 Outline **two** reasons why rapid urbanisation leads to problems in many LIC cities. *(4)*

10 Outline **two** reasons why urban land use tends to be segregated rather than mixed together. *(4)*

11 Outline **two** characteristics of shanty towns. *(4)*

12 Describe the changing fortunes of inner-city areas. *(4)*

13 Study **Figure 6.11**. Using this figure and your own knowledge, explain the factors that contribute to counterurbanisation. *(6)*

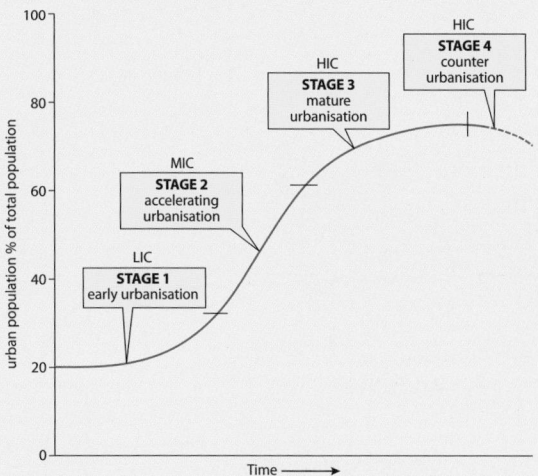

Figure 6.11

14 Explain the advantages and disadvantages of brownfield sites. *(6)*

15 Discuss the strategies used to improve living conditions in a shanty town in a named city. *(9)*

Exam Section C question

16 Why would a transect through different urban areas used to measure environmental quality need to sample more than one or two sites? *(4)*

Chapter 7: Fragile environments

Fragile environments and sustainability

Make sure you know and understand this key term:

- **Sustainability**: actions that meet the needs of the present without reducing the ability of future generations to meet their needs.

> The focus of this chapter is **soil erosion**, **desertification** and **deforestation**. These are not the only ways in which natural environments are being made more fragile, but they are very important ones.

> It is the growth of the world's population that most threatens to disturb the fragile balance of environments. Humans have disturbed 90 per cent of the Earth's land surface to some degree.

Fragile environments are environments that are under threat from change, damage or unsustainable use. Fragile environments are either very sensitive to the presence of humans, or they have been made fragile by large-scale exploitation by humans.

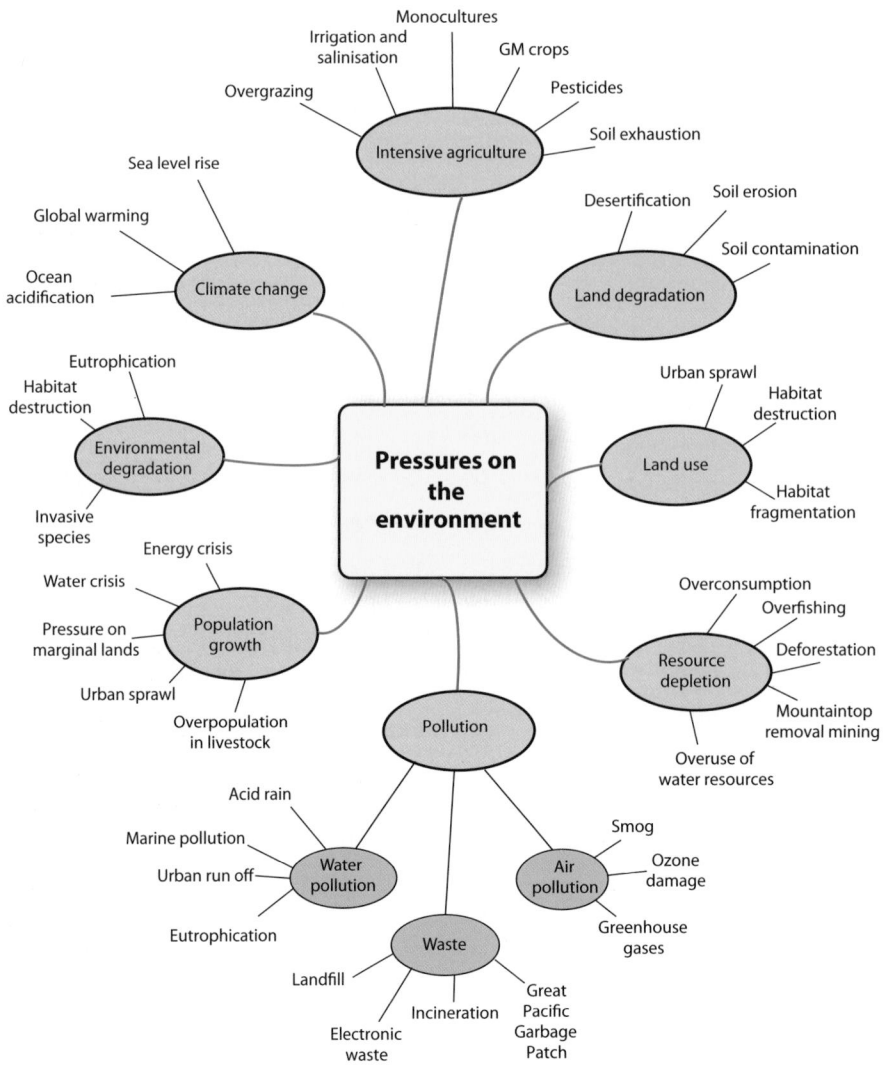

Figure 7.1 *Some of the pressures on environments*

Soil erosion and desertification

> Soil erosion is the washing away or blowing away of topsoil, which greatly reduces the fertility of the remaining soil. It is a natural process but is made worse by human activity.

There are three main types of **soil erosion**:

- sheet erosion – moderate rainfall removes topsoil from bare soil slopes
- gully erosion – intense rainfall cuts gullies into slopes
- wind erosion – in dry conditions, loose dry soil is blown away.

Soil erosion is made worse by:

- cutting down or clearing the vegetation that protects the soil
- overgrazing – animals remove the vegetation protecting the soil
- overcultivating the soil – weakens soil structure, making it easier to erode
- compacting the soil with heavy machinery – increases run off
- ploughing fields in the same direction as the slope – increases gullying.

Desertification

Make sure you know and understand this key term:

- **Desertification**: the spread of desert-like conditions into semi-arid areas.

Desertification is a natural process but is made worse by human activity.

- Little rainfall (drought) reduces vegetation cover, increasing soil erosion.
- More intense rainfall increases run off and reduces soil moisture.

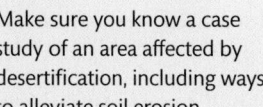

TOP TIP
Make sure you know a case study of an area affected by desertification, including ways to alleviate soil erosion.

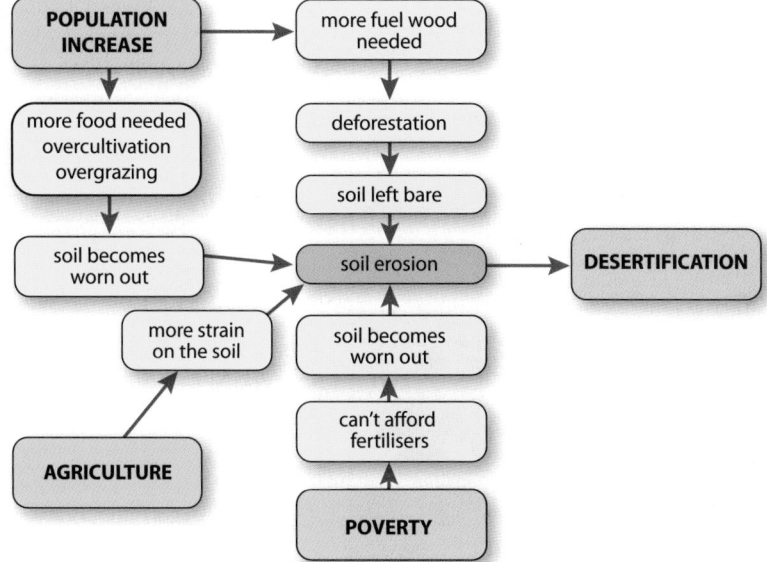

Figure 7.2 *Human causes of desertification*

The Sahel is a good example of desertification. Until the 1960s there was plenty of water, crops and livestock did well. Then an increase in population meant more pressure on the land. People cleared trees for fuel and building material. Overcultivation and overgrazing removed vegetation cover. Soil was quickly eroded by wind and water erosion.

Consequences and management of soil erosion

The consequences of soil erosion are all negative. The loss of farmland and the reduction in food production can have very serious consequences in poorer areas:

- **malnutrition**

- **famine** and starvation

- **migration** – refugees try to escape famine by going somewhere else.

In poorer areas of the world, international aid efforts are then required to try to reduce the impact of the famine and save people's lives.

Famines became common in the Sahel as a result of desertification. Thousands of people have died. International food aid has saved lives but it has not done anything to reduce soil erosion.

Management

Desertification is a very difficult process to reverse while rainfall remains low. There is some evidence that when rainfall increases, the fragile semi-arid environment can start to recover.

Management of soil erosion is all about preventing further erosion from happening.

- Planting trees and shrubs can reduce wind speeds to reduce wind erosion.

- Terracing and contour-ploughing reduces soil erosion down slopes.

- Increasing vegetation cover and mulching soil protects it from heavy rain.

- Small dams in streams or existing gullies can reduce the speed of water and reduce water erosion.

- Building lines of stones or earth walls along contours reduces run off and helps keep more water in the soil.

Organic farming and permaculture both reduce soil erosion. Organic farming uses animal manure and manure crops to keep the soil fertile and well structured. Permaculture mixes food and tree crops, which ensures the ground surface is well covered.

One successful management technique in the Sahel has been to build small stone walls that follow the slope of the land. These act as dams when it rains, stopping surface water run off and increasing infiltration.

Figure 7.3 *Turkmenistan: a grid of vegetation is being used to stabilise the soil*

Causes of deforestation

Make sure you know and understand this key term:

- **Deforestation**: the felling and clearing of forested lands by humans.

> While most primary forests in temperate countries have been cleared over the centuries, tropical rain forests have only recently started to be cut down – at an alarming rate. Since 1990 half the world's rainforests have already been cleared.

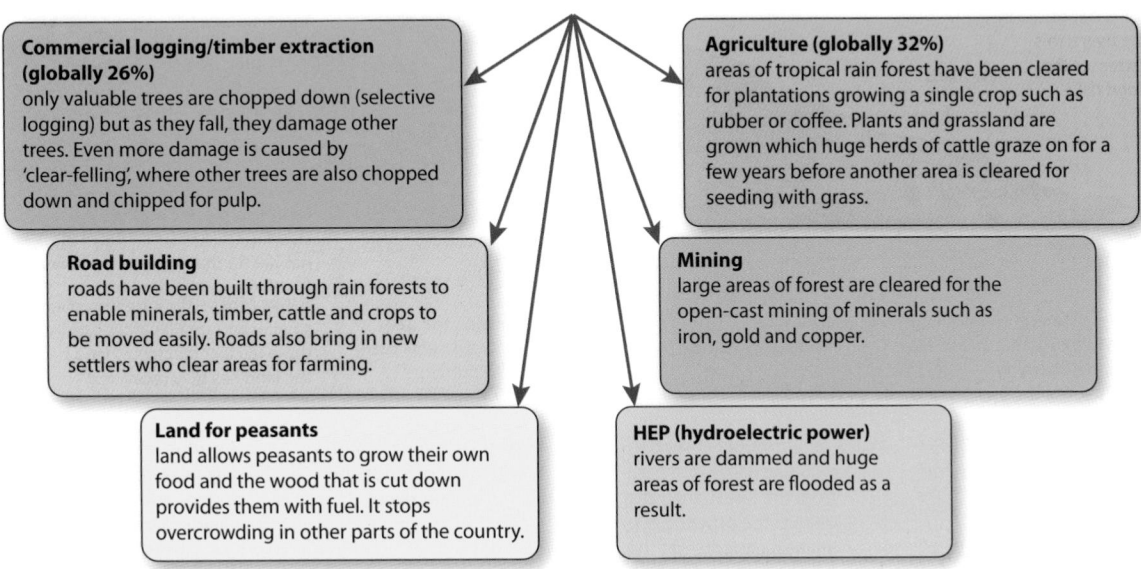

Why are rainforests being cut down?

Commercial logging/timber extraction (globally 26%)
only valuable trees are chopped down (selective logging) but as they fall, they damage other trees. Even more damage is caused by 'clear-felling', where other trees are also chopped down and chipped for pulp.

Agriculture (globally 32%)
areas of tropical rain forest have been cleared for plantations growing a single crop such as rubber or coffee. Plants and grassland are grown which huge herds of cattle graze on for a few years before another area is cleared for seeding with grass.

Road building
roads have been built through rain forests to enable minerals, timber, cattle and crops to be moved easily. Roads also bring in new settlers who clear areas for farming.

Mining
large areas of forest are cleared for the open-cast mining of minerals such as iron, gold and copper.

Land for peasants
land allows peasants to grow their own food and the wood that is cut down provides them with fuel. It stops overcrowding in other parts of the country.

HEP (hydroelectric power)
rivers are dammed and huge areas of forest are flooded as a result.

Figure 7.4 *Causes of rainforest deforestation*

Large-scale deforestation in the Amazon rainforest has many different causes, including:

- mining – for example the iron ore mine at Carajas in the Amazon Basin
- road building – for example the Trans-Amazonian Highway in Brazil
- logging for timber exports – for example teak and mahogany in the Amazon Basin
- huge cattle ranches and other large-scale agricultural uses – especially soya cultivation and biofuel crops
- reservoirs and dams for HEP schemes – for example Itaipu, Tucurui and the Xingu complex.

TOP TIP
Make sure you know a case study of an area of threatened tropical rainforest and the causes of its deforestation.

Global issues (Section D)

Consequences of deforestation

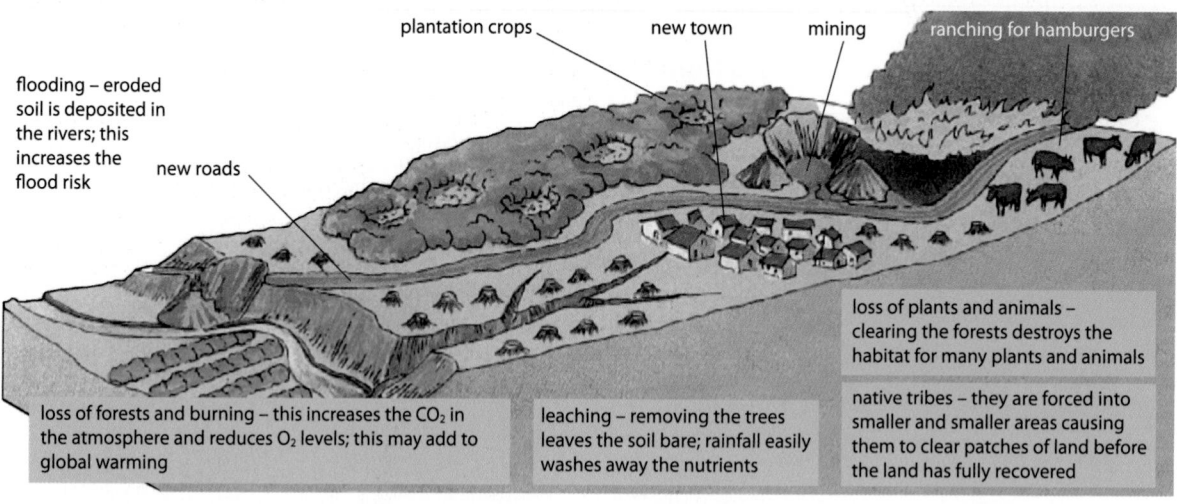

Countries such as Brazil have gained economically from exploiting the goods and services of the rainforest, in the same ways that HICs benefitted from clearing their forests over the centuries

Biodiversity is lost as habitats for animals, birds and insects are destroyed. A wide variety of medicinal plants are also lost

Forests absorb carbon dioxide from the air and deforestation means this doesn't happen. So deforestation is contributing to the build up of greenhouse gases

plantation crops   new town   mining   ranching for hamburgers

flooding – eroded soil is deposited in the rivers; this increases the flood risk

new roads

loss of plants and animals – clearing the forests destroys the habitat for many plants and animals

loss of forests and burning – this increases the CO_2 in the atmosphere and reduces O_2 levels; this may add to global warming

leaching – removing the trees leaves the soil bare; rainfall easily washes away the nutrients

native tribes – they are forced into smaller and smaller areas causing them to clear patches of land before the land has fully recovered

Roads open up more areas of the rainforest for development

When loggers take the valuable hardwood trees from the forest, they also clear all the other trees to make it easier to get the timber out of the area

Open-cast mining destroys large areas of forest and pollutes rivers

Clearing land for cattle not only releases carbon dioxide as trees are burned, but also leads to soil nutrient loss and soil erosion

Figure 7.5 *Some consequences of deforestation of the Amazon rainforest*

While many of the consequences of tropical rainforest deforestation are negative (loss of biodiversity, contribution to **global warming**), there are some positive consequences too, such as a contribution to economic development in LICs.

Managing rainforests in a sustainable way

The key to sustainable management is using resources now in a way that ensures that future generations will still be able to use the same resources to meet their needs.

protection – national parks and reserves prevent development or only allow very little

careful planning and control of logging

selective logging of valuable trees only

replanting of felled areas

restrictions on the number of logging licences issued

developing alternative energy sources to reduce reliance on wood for fuel

agroforestry – combining crops and trees together on the same land (either growing crops amongst the forest or growing trees on cropland)

substitution – finding alternative sources for the resources being taken out of the rainforest

Figure 7.6 *How can the Amazon rainforest be used in a sustainable way?*

International cooperation

Concerted international cooperation is the only way to ensure the tropical rainforest has a future.

- International programmes, such as the UN Forum on Forests (UNFF), promote sustainable forest management around the world.

- International treaties aim to protect rainforest ecosystems with international agreements. CITES is a treaty that protects endangered species that are traded, and the International Tropical Timber Agreement (ITTA) (2006) aims to promote sustainable forest management and the sale of sustainable timber products.

- International pressure groups such as Greenpeace monitor deforestation and help track down illegal loggers.

TOP TIP

Make sure you know a case study of an area of threatened tropical rainforest and how it is managed in a sustainable way.

Causes of global warming and climate change

On average, global land temperatures are 1°C higher now than they were at the end of the 19th century.

The Earth's climate has changed many times over the millennia. Global temperatures have warmed and cooled many times. These changes were due to natural causes.

Natural causes of climate change

- Orbit wobbles – the Earth's orbit changes once every 100,000 years (called Milankovitch cycles).
- Sun output changes – the Sun gives out more or less radiated heat energy over an 11 year cycle.
- Volcanoes – major eruptions pump ash into the atmosphere which has a big cooling effect.
- Ocean current changes – warming or cooling ocean currents sometimes shift.

While some think that natural causes are again the reason for the current rise in global temperatures, most experts agree that natural causes, such as variations in the Sun's output or a decline in volcanic activity, are not sufficient to explain the temperature rise. Increasing greenhouse gas emissions do explain the rise, and most experts agree that human activity is the cause of these.

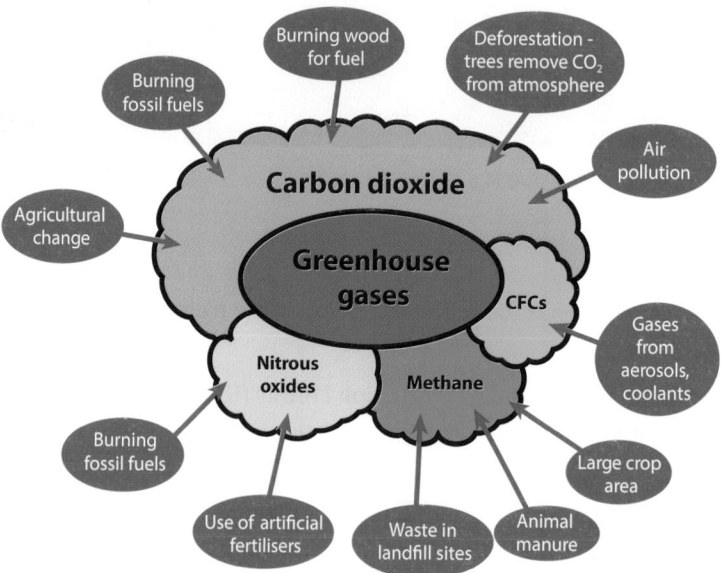

Figure 7.7 *Human causes of greenhouse gas emissions*

Make sure you know and understand these key terms:

- **Global warming**: a slow but significant rise in the Earth's temperature.
- **Enhanced greenhouse effect**: the warming of the Earth's atmosphere because pollution is preventing heat from escaping into space.

HICs are the main producers of greenhouse gases. The USA is responsible for 36 per cent of all greenhouse gases.

Consequences of global warming and climate change

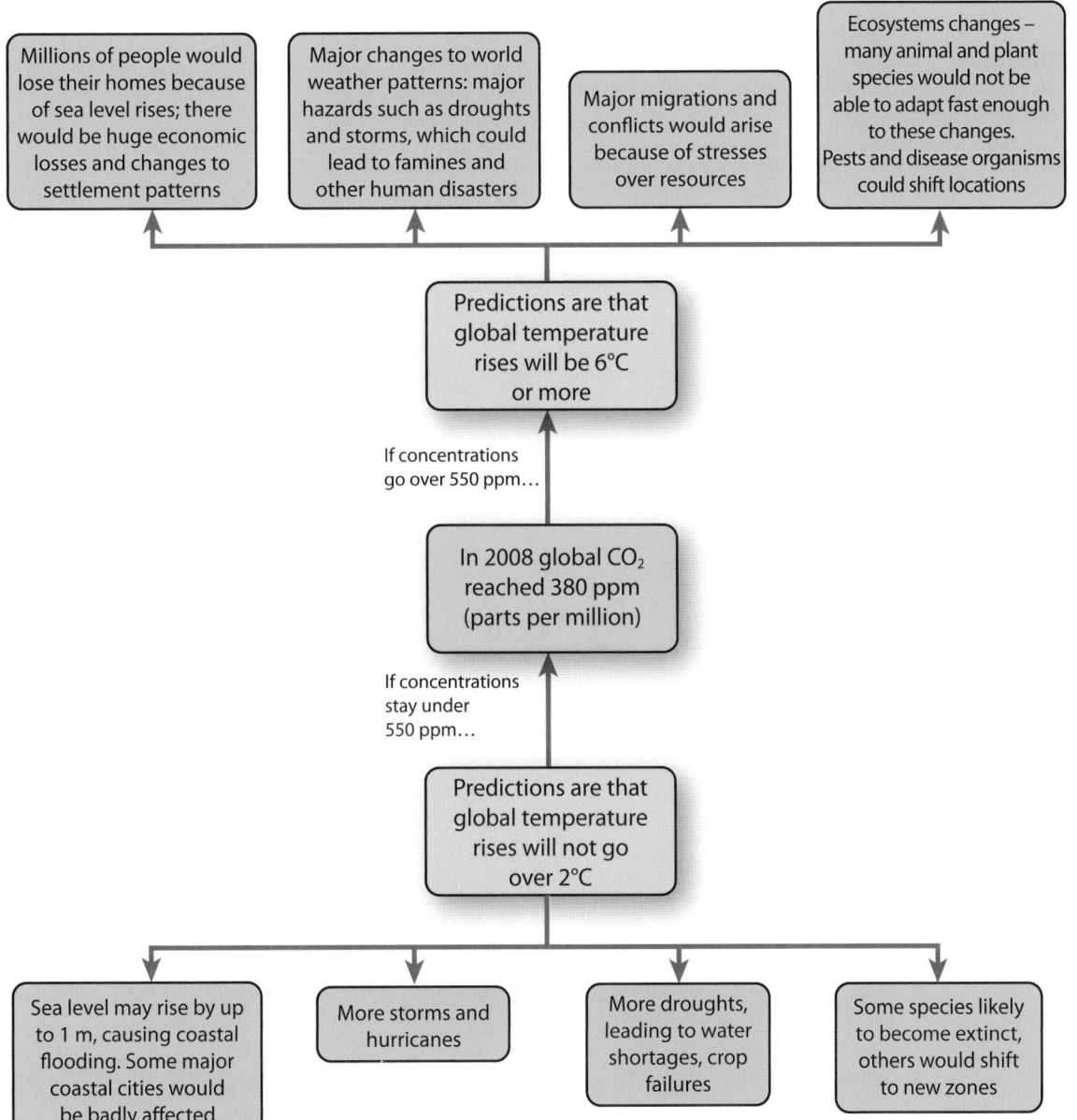

Millions of people would lose their homes because of sea level rises; there would be huge economic losses and changes to settlement patterns

Major changes to world weather patterns: major hazards such as droughts and storms, which could lead to famines and other human disasters

Major migrations and conflicts would arise because of stresses over resources

Ecosystems changes – many animal and plant species would not be able to adapt fast enough to these changes. Pests and disease organisms could shift locations

Predictions are that global temperature rises will be 6°C or more

If concentrations go over 550 ppm…

In 2008 global CO_2 reached 380 ppm (parts per million)

If concentrations stay under 550 ppm…

Predictions are that global temperature rises will not go over 2°C

Sea level may rise by up to 1 m, causing coastal flooding. Some major coastal cities would be badly affected

More storms and hurricanes

More droughts, leading to water shortages, crop failures

Some species likely to become extinct, others would shift to new zones

Figure 7.8 *Consequences of global warming and climate change will differ depending on the scale of the temperature rise*

There are positive consequences to global warming and climate change too: some countries will be able to grow a wider range of crops. Resources previously buried under ice will become accessible, such as oil.

Consequences of global warming and climate change in Bangladesh: case study

TOP TIP ✓

Make sure you know a case study of the threats posed by global warming and climate change to one country. The textbook uses Tuvalu and Bangladesh for this; you may have studied a different example.

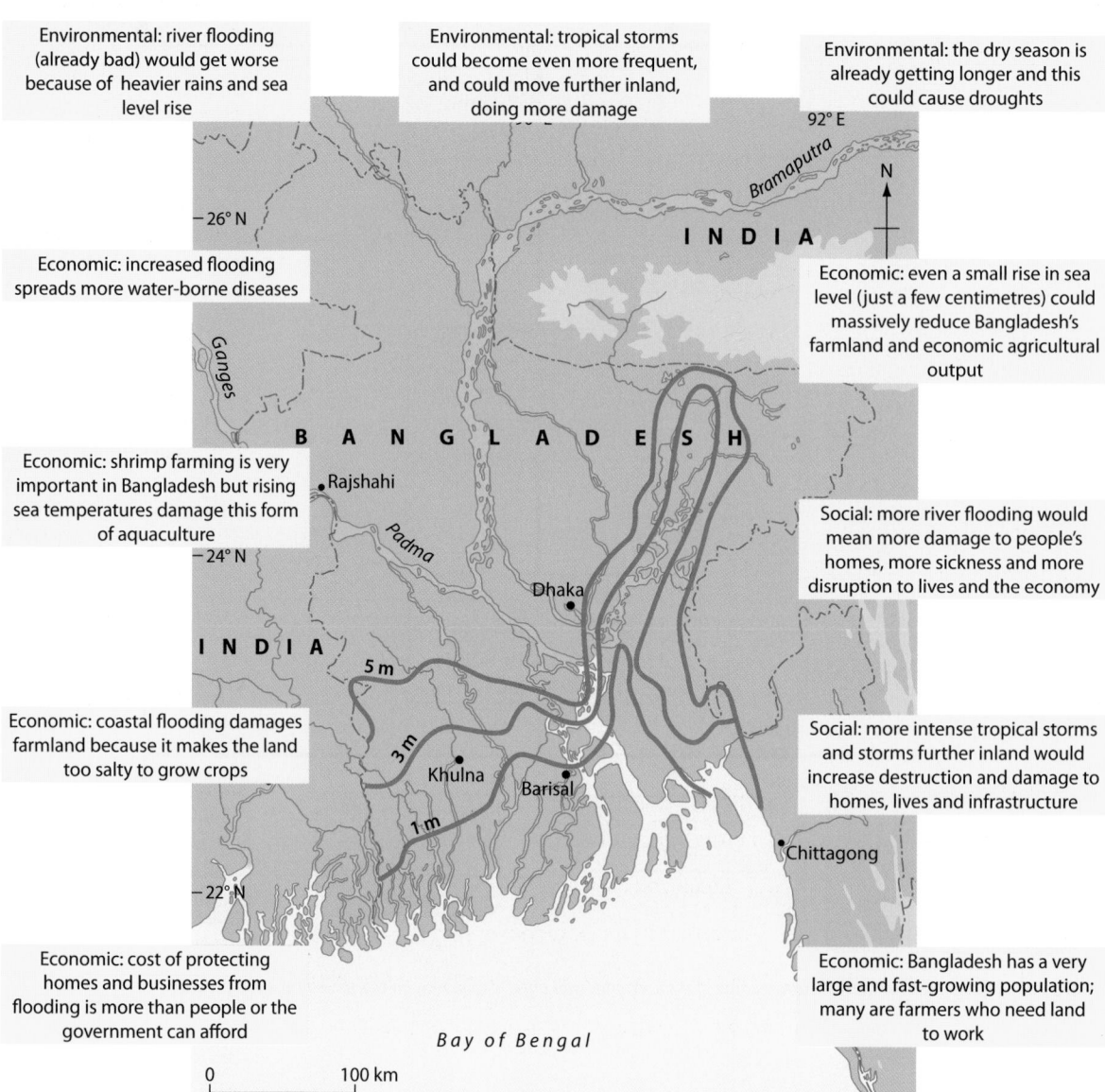

Environmental: river flooding (already bad) would get worse because of heavier rains and sea level rise

Environmental: tropical storms could become even more frequent, and could move further inland, doing more damage

Environmental: the dry season is already getting longer and this could cause droughts

Economic: increased flooding spreads more water-borne diseases

Economic: even a small rise in sea level (just a few centimetres) could massively reduce Bangladesh's farmland and economic agricultural output

Economic: shrimp farming is very important in Bangladesh but rising sea temperatures damage this form of aquaculture

Social: more river flooding would mean more damage to people's homes, more sickness and more disruption to lives and the economy

Economic: coastal flooding damages farmland because it makes the land too salty to grow crops

Social: more intense tropical storms and storms further inland would increase destruction and damage to homes, lives and infrastructure

Economic: cost of protecting homes and businesses from flooding is more than people or the government can afford

Economic: Bangladesh has a very large and fast-growing population; many are farmers who need land to work

Figure 7.9 *Consequences of global warming and climate change for Bangladesh. The dark red lines indicate possible future coastlines*

Global issues (Section D)

Managing the causes of global warming and climate change

Ways to reduce greenhouse gas emissions would include:

- reduce our use of fossil fuels – for example by levying fines on industries for creating emissions

- find alternative energy sources to replace fossil fuels

- reduce deforestation and increase afforestation

- develop carbon capture technologies.

International cooperation

- Kyoto Protocol (1997) – global agreement to cut emissions of CO_2 by 2012. Only 38 countries signed and few met their targets.

- Copenhagen Accord (2009) – a new agreement that softened the terms of Kyoto. Countries were asked to say what cuts they would be able to make to CO_2 emissions by 2020.

- Opposition from LICs – they do not see why they should slow down their economic development to clean up a problem HICs created.

Alternative energy sources

There are advantages and disadvantages to current alternative energy sources:

- wind farms, tidal barrages, solar panels, wave power generators – produce clean energy but relative small amounts of it and not all the time

- nuclear power – produces large amount of power all the time, but with potential for radiation leaks or terrorist attacks

- hydroelectric power – produces large amounts of power all the time, but needs particular physical geography.

Adapting to global warming and climate change

- Rising sea levels – either have to build defences or move inland.

- More hazards – improve ability to predict and prepare for them.

- Ecosystem changes – open up new areas for development.

- Health – improve medical treatment of those diseases that are likely to spread.

- Conflict – international cooperation to defuse conflicts over scarce resources.

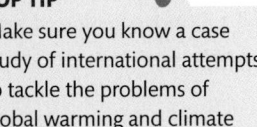

TOP TIP

Make sure you know a case study of international attempts to tackle the problems of global warming and climate change.

Kyoto also set up a Clean Development Mechanism (CDM):

- countries that beat their emissions targets get carbon credits that they can sell to other countries

- countries that help poorer countries beat emission targets also get credits.

Global issues (Section D)

1   Which of the following gives the best definition of sustainability? **(1)**

   a) the process that has created a more connected world, bringing together trade, population movements and flows of aid and information

   b) the measure of the mark humans make on the natural world

   c) actions that meet the needs of the present without reducing the ability of future generations to meet their needs

2   Is desertification a natural process or something only humans create? **(1)**

3   Name a greenhouse gas. **(1)**

4   What is the name of the international agreement that required countries to cut greenhouse emissions by an average of 5 per cent by 2012? **(1)**

5   Define the term 'desertification'. **(2)**

6   Give **two** examples of the consequences of soil erosion. **(2)**

7   Give **two** examples of the consequences of tropical rainforest deforestation. **(2)**

8   Give **two** examples of the consequences of global warming and climate change. **(2)**

9   Outline **two** reasons for an increase in soil erosion on cultivated land. **(4)**

10 Outline **two** reasons why rainforests are being cut down. **(4)**

11 Outline how the enhanced greenhouse effect leads to global warming. **(4)**

12 Describe **two** ways in which humans could adapt to the consequences of global warming and climate change. **(4)**

13 Study **Figure 7.10**. Using this figure and your own knowledge, explain the factors that contribute to the increase in global carbon dioxide emissions. **(6)**

14 Discuss the strategies used to reduce soil erosion in LICs. **(6)**

15 Discuss the problems associated with international attempts to tackle the problems of global warming and climate change. Refer to a named example or examples of international agreement(s) in your answer. **(9)**

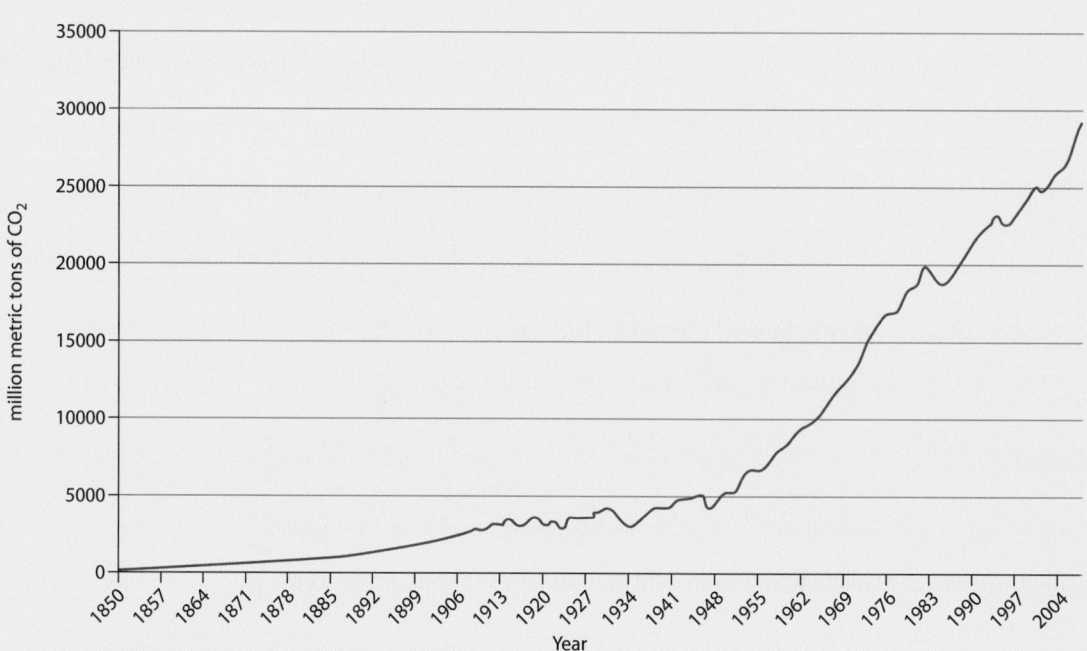

Source: Marland et. al (2007) Global, Regional, and National CO_2 Emissions.
In Trends: A Compendium of Data on Global Change. CDIAC U.S.A

Figure 7.10 *Global carbon dioxide emissions, 1850–2005*

Chapter 8: Globalisation and migration

The rise of the global economy

Make sure you know and understand this key term:

- **Globalisation**: the process that has created a more connected world, with increases in the movements of goods (trade) and people (migration and tourism) worldwide.

Today there is scarcely a country in the world that does not take part in the global economy in some way.

cotton grown in Egypt

cloth woven in Thailand

synthetic fibre made in China

buttons and zips made in India

jeans made in Bangladesh

jeans shipped to Rotterdam (The Netherlands)

trousers delivered to UK shops

Figure 8.1 *The production chain of a pair of jeans*

One indication that we are increasingly part of the global economy is the international **production chains** that create and supply the products we buy. Each stage adds value to the final product, but the company that oversees the chain sources each stage in the country that offers it most cheaply.

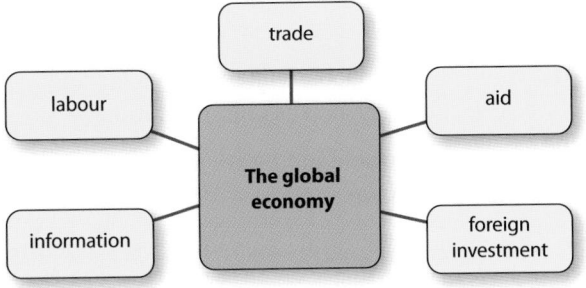

trade

labour

aid

The global economy

information

foreign investment

(Labour involves both migrants moving to find work and TNCs moving to find cheap labour.)

Figure 8.2 *Five factors in the rise of the global economy*

The global shift in manufacturing

> The location of manufacturing has been shifting from HICs to MICs and LICs. This process creates deindustrialisation in the HICs and industrialisation in MICs and LICs.

The global shift in manufacturing has happened because TNCs want to locate their manufacturing processes to create the most profit. Developing countries often have four key advantages here:

1. cheap labour and/or labour that isn't unionised

2. cheap land for building big new factories

3. weak laws controlling pollution or carbon emissions

4. proximity to a cheap raw material source or other resources.

The container revolution has also been very important. Because all goods are now moved around the world in identical containers, the machinery required to move the containers can be standardised. Ports can operate very efficiently and quickly, and costs can therefore come right down.

Figure 8.3 *Containers being loaded onto a ship*

TOP TIP ✓

Make sure you know a case study of India and China's changing role in the global economy with the reasons for the changes and their consequences.

China and India: changing roles in the global economy

The winners of the global shift in manufacturing have been countries such as China and India.

- Together, China and India have 40 per cent of the world's population.

- China is now the world's second biggest economy, India is in tenth place.

- It is only 50 years since both were very poor, rural countries.

China and India – key advantages for global manufacturing:

- cheap labour

- limits on working hours weakly enforced

- health and safety regulations weakly enforced

- restrictions on strikes and unions

- tax incentives and tax-free zones

Transnational corporations

Make sure you know and understand this key term:

- **TNC**: Transnational corporation – a company that has operations (factories, offices, R&D, shops) in more than one country. Many TNCs are large and have well-known brands.

> TNCs are a key force in globalisation. Their production chains link raw materials with manufacturing locations, manufacturing locations with research and development centres, and products with markets all across the globe.

Benefits and costs to countries hosting TNCs

Benefits	Costs
TNCs bring money, modern technology and skills to poorer countries	TNCs often pay low wages and expect long hours
The country's infrastructure (roads, energy supplies, etc.) is improved by TNCs or for TNCs	TNC jobs are often boring, repetitive and don't develop many skills
TNCs create jobs, people can buy more and pay more tax	Most of the profits go back to the TNC's base in a rich country
TNCs in manufacturing industries create exports for the country, so it can earn foreign currency	TNCs often take very little care to protect the environment unless laws say they have to
Multiplier effect – other industries can grow up around TNC factories	TNCs can leave a country if somewhere else becomes more profitable

TOP TIP

Make sure you know a case study of the global operations of a TNC or a TNC's operations in one LIC.

Walmart: the TNC

Walmart is a TNC with its headquarters in the USA. In 2012 its different operations around the world brought in $4.5 billion.

Walmart's strategy is to sell a wide range of products at low prices

Walmart has 8,500 stores around the world, in 27 different countries

Many of the products are cheap because they are made in developing countries where wages are low

Around the world, 2.2 million people work for Walmart

Figure 8.4 *Walmart owns the Seiyu chain of supermarkets in Japan*

The growth of global tourism

Tourism is one of the fastest growing global industries. Around 900 million people become international tourists each year.

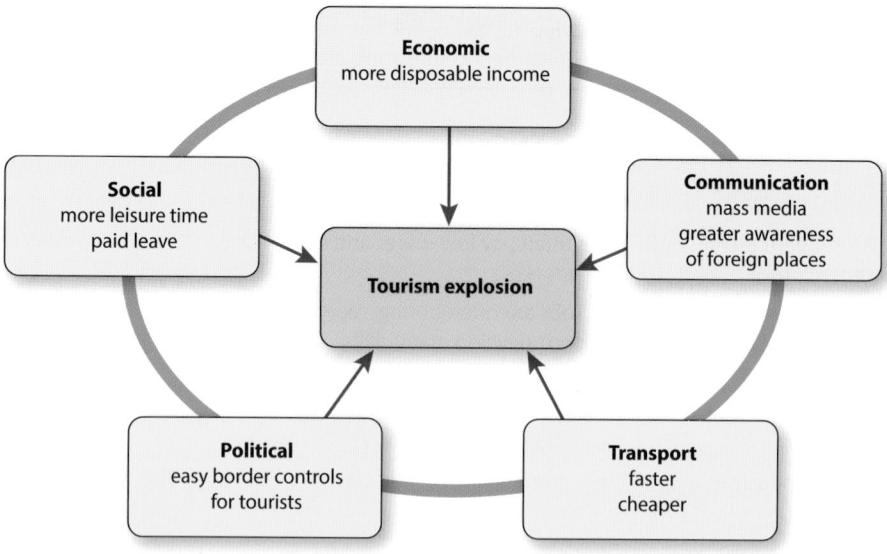

Figure 8.5 *Main causes of the tourism explosion*

The huge increase in the numbers of tourists moving around the world is a direct consequence of globalisation but it has also been a cause of globalisation as different parts of the world become more dependent on tourism in their economies.

There are five main causes for the growth in global tourism.

Each year, more people in MICs and LICs have the disposable income and holiday time required to become tourists. Each year, more money is spent by governments in promoting their countries as tourist destinations.

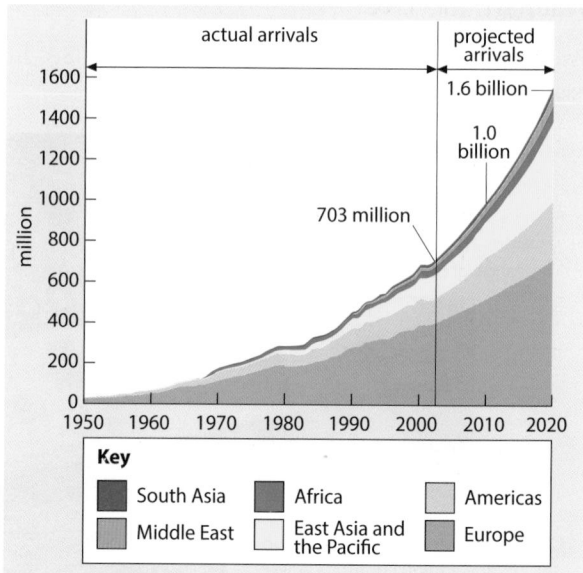

Figure 8.6 *World tourist arrivals by region, 1950–2020*

The impacts of mass tourism

Make sure you know and understand this key term:

- **Mass tourism**: popular, large-scale tourism of the kind that started in southern Europe, the Caribbean and North America in the 1960s and 1970s.

> Mass tourism can have both positive impacts and negative impacts on the economy, the environment and the people of destination areas.

Economic impacts $$$

- Brings money into the country's economy
- Money often goes to big businesses and not to local ones
- Creates jobs for local people
- Jobs for locals are often low paid and seasonal
- Brings new infrastructure to the region
- Mass tourism can cause traffic congestion, which affects local businesses

Environmental impacts

- Can increase awareness of need for nature conservation areas
- Local environment can become bulldozed and concreted over
- Money from tourism can help pay to protect and repair the environment
- Tourism creates local pollution problems
- Tourism may actually help preserve key areas or species. For example, boat trips to see sea life
- Tourist activity can directly damage the environment. Air travel means massive CO_2 emissions

Impacts on societies and cultures

- Helps revive local skills and local handicrafts
- Tourists' behaviour (drinking, etc.) can offend local people
- Cultural tourism values people's cultural heritage
- Tourist centres also encourage crime, prostitution
- Brings people together from all over the world
- Can erode the local language as people increasingly rely on global languages such as English

1 Which of the following gives the best definition of globalisation? *(1)*

   a) the increasing industrialisation of poorer countries

   b) the process that has created a more connected world

   c) the comparative advantages granted by locations in cheaper countries.

2 What do the letters TNC stand for? *(1)*

3 What is meant by 'mass tourism'? *(1)*

4 Give **one** example of an ecotourism destination. *(1)*

5 Give **two** reasons for the global shift in manufacturing from HICs to LICs. *(2)*

6 Define the term 'production chain'. *(2)*

7 Name **two** positive impacts of the development of mass tourism. *(2)*

8 Define the term 'asylum seeker'. *(2)*

9 Outline **two** reasons why call centres for UK companies have been located in countries such as India and the Philippines. *(4)*

10 Outline **two** reasons why mass tourism often has negative environmental impacts. *(4)*

11 Outline **two** characteristics of ecotourism. *(4)*

12 Describe the reasons why governments might want to encourage more migrants to enter their country. *(4)*

13 Study **Figure 8.12**. Using this figure and your own knowledge, explain the factors that contribute to the growth in global tourism. *(6)*

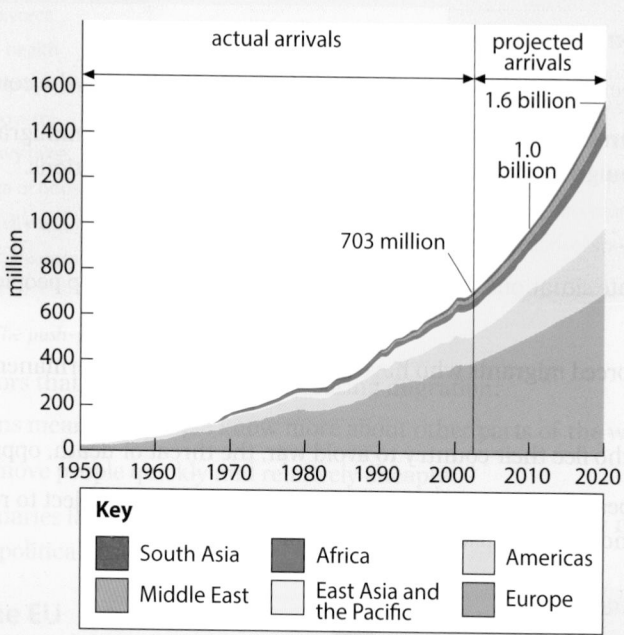

Figure 8.12

Chapter 9: Development and human welfare

The nature of development

Economic development is key to a country's progress, but development also has many other strands, for example:

- social development – such as equal opportunities for men and women

- political development – such as an adult's right to vote

- demographic development – such as rising life expectancy.

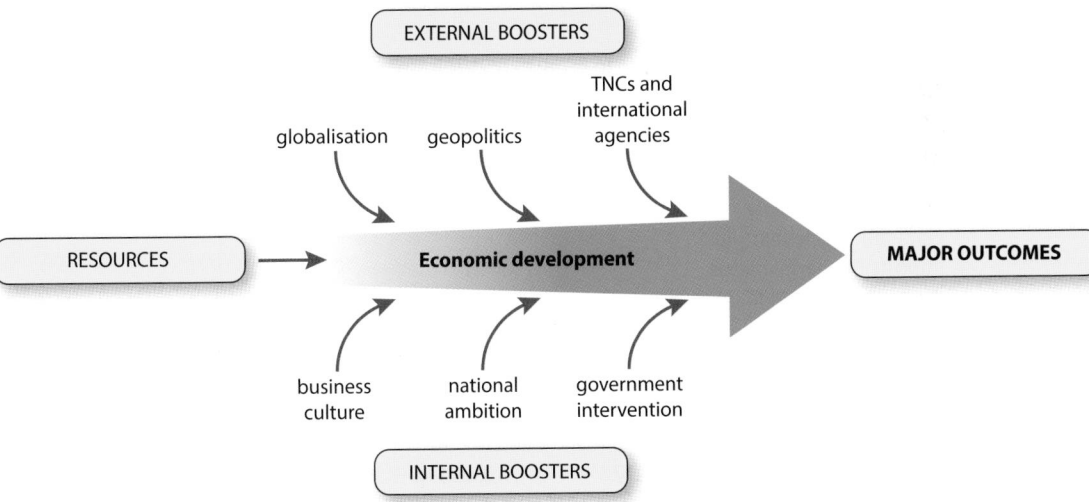

Resources: get development moving. Physical resources, such as soils, climate and mineral wealth, are used by human resources, such as entrepreneurs, skilled workers

External boosters: come from outside the country, for example a booming global economy, trade blocs, TNCs

Figure 9.1 *Factors generating economic development*

Internal boosters: such things as government incentives, business culture, etc., which come from within a country

Major outcomes: the outcomes of development, such as rising living standards, sectoral shifts (see page 31), environmental impacts

Development indicators

Development indicator	What does it measure?	Example of a HIC (year)	Example of a LIC (year)
Per capita GDP (gross domestic product)	The total value of a country's economic production over the course of a year, divided by the number of people in the country	USA $47,500 (2011)	Haiti $1300 (2011)
Per capita GNI (gross national income)	The total value of a country's economic production plus net income received from abroad over a year, divided by the number of people living in the country	Norway $88,890 (2011)	Uganda $510 (2011)
Employment per sector	The number of people employed in the primary, secondary and tertiary sectors (see page 31). LICs are dominated by their primary sectors, HICs by their tertiary sectors	Austria 5% of adults employed in agriculture; 68% in services (2008)	Ethiopia 75% of adults employed in agriculture; 20% in services (2008)
Energy consumption	Measured in different ways but a common one is the amount of electricity generated each year plus imports of energy minus exports, measured in kilowatt-hours (kWh)	Japan 859.7 trillion kWh (2011)	Congo 534 million kWh (2008)
Birth rate	Often measured as the number of births per 1000 people per year	Germany 8.33 (2012)	Niger 50.06 (2012)
Death rate	Often measured as the number of deaths per 1000 people per year	Italy 9.94 (2012)	Zambia 12.42 (2012)
Infant mortality rate	The number of deaths of infants under one year old per year, per 1000 live births in the same year	UK 4.56 (2012)	Mali 109.08 (2012)
Life expectancy	The average number of years that a group of people born in the same year can expect to live	Australia 81.9 (2012)	Namibia 52.17 (2012)

TOP TIP

Make sure you know about the following development indicators:

- **per capita GDP/GNI**
- employment by sector
- energy consumption
- birth, death and infant mortality rates
- life expectancy.

Each indicator has advantages and disadvantages.

- For example, per capita GNI is useful for comparing countries, but because it is an average it is not possible to tell if a very few people in a country are enormously wealthy while most are very poor.

- Death rates might be high if a country is at war or has a culture that means men are encouraged to drink a lot of alcohol (e.g. Russia).

Quality of life and its indicators

Quality of life and standard of living

- Standard of living is an economic measure. Does a person have enough money to live on?

- **Quality of life** is a social measure. Do people have a long and healthy life? Are people satisfied? Do they feel safe and secure? Are they happy?

Quality of life indicators

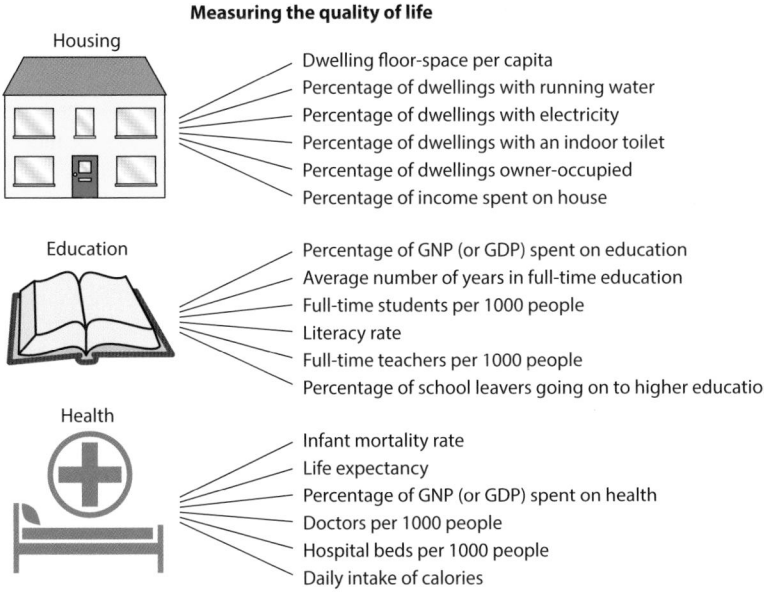

Measuring the quality of life

Housing
- Dwelling floor-space per capita
- Percentage of dwellings with running water
- Percentage of dwellings with electricity
- Percentage of dwellings with an indoor toilet
- Percentage of dwellings owner-occupied
- Percentage of income spent on house

Education
- Percentage of GNP (or GDP) spent on education
- Average number of years in full-time education
- Full-time students per 1000 people
- Literacy rate
- Full-time teachers per 1000 people
- Percentage of school leavers going on to higher education

Health
- Infant mortality rate
- Life expectancy
- Percentage of GNP (or GDP) spent on health
- Doctors per 1000 people
- Hospital beds per 1000 people
- Daily intake of calories

Figure 9.2 *Some quality of life indicators*

HDI

The Human Development Index (**HDI**) combines three development indicators:

- per capita income
- **literacy**
- **life expectancy**.

The HDI is the average of the scores achieved by a country in those three fields. HDI scores range from 0 to 1. The higher the HDI, the higher the level of development and the quality of life.

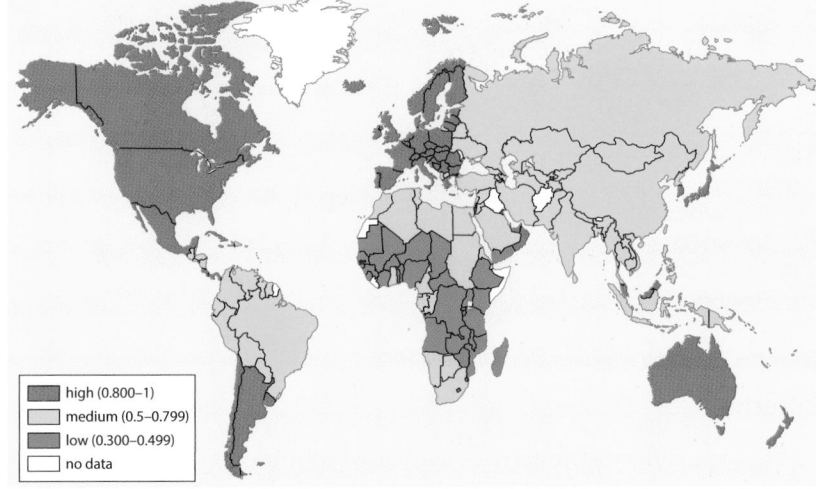

high (0.800–1)
medium (0.5–0.799)
low (0.300–0.499)
no data

Figure 9.3 *The Human Development Index (HDI)*

Levels of economic development

Although every country's development path is different, geographers put countries into different categories to see global patterns of development.

There are different classifications; the one used on this course is based on GNI per capita, which divides the countries into:

- LICs – lower income countries
- MICs – middle income countries
- HICs – high income countries.

The World Bank uses this classification system too. It divides MICs into two subgroups – Upper MICs and Lower MICs.

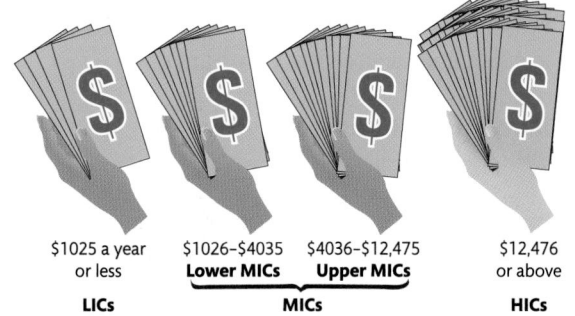

$1025 a year or less	$1026–$4035 **Lower MICs**	$4036–$12,475 **Upper MICs**	$12,476 or above
LICs	**MICs**		**HICs**

Figure 9.4 *LICs, MICs and HICs (using 2011 GNI per capita figures)*

In 2012, the World Bank classified 36 countries as LICs, 54 as Lower MICs, 54 as Higher MICs and 70 countries as HICs.

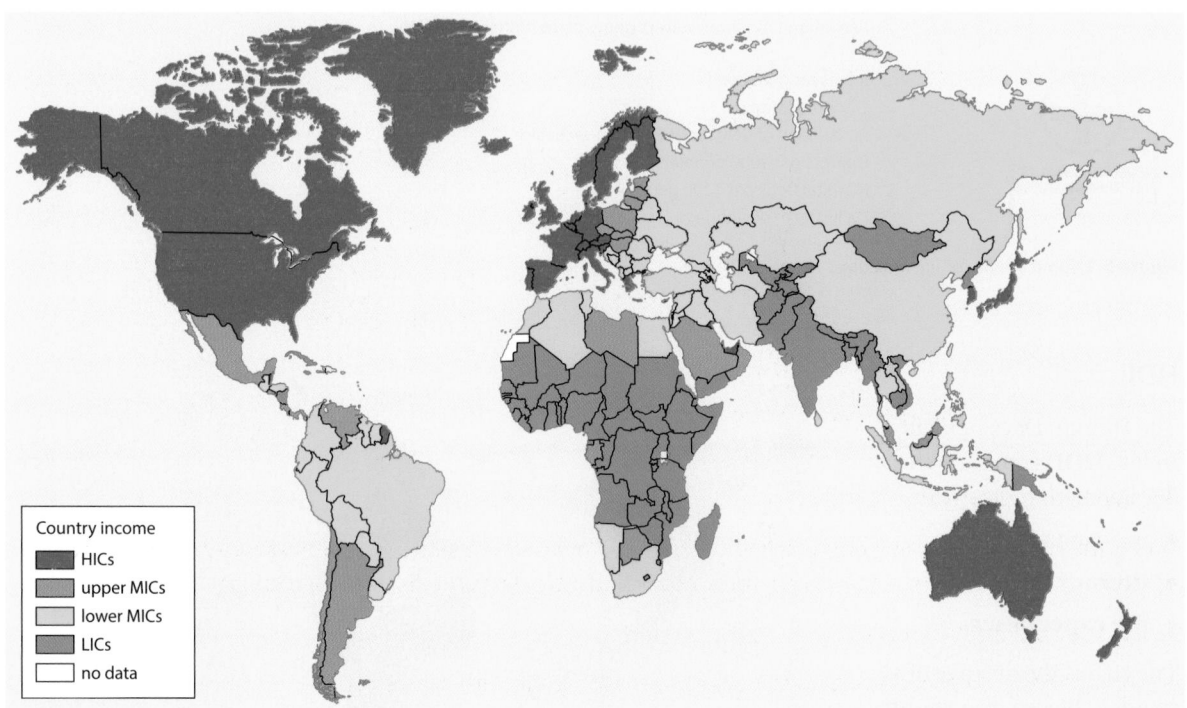

Country income
- HICs
- upper MICs
- lower MICs
- LICs
- no data

Figure 9.5 *The global pattern of LICs, MICs and HICs*

Patterns

- HICs are mainly the western industrialised countries.
- Most LICs are in Africa; GNI per capita makes India an LIC too.
- MICs are a difficult category to deal with. China's development is very different from Ecuador's or South Africa's, for example.

The changing patterns of global development

Make sure you know and understand these key terms:

- **Emerging economies**: countries that were poor but are now getting richer very quickly.

- NIC: newly industrialised countries (e.g. South Korea, Malaysia).

- BRIC: **B**razil, **R**ussia, **I**ndia and **C**hina: four countries that dominate the newly industrialised category.

- **Development gap**: the difference between countries with the lowest development indicators and those with the highest.

> Ten years ago, HICs dominated the world economy, producing 75 per cent of the world's GDP. In 2012 the International Monetary Fund (IMF) predicted that LICs and MICs would out-produce HICs in 2013.

New industrialisation

Globalisation has powered the rise of the BRICs and other NICs. China is a great example. It has become a global manufacturing powerhouse because of a combination of external and internal boosters:

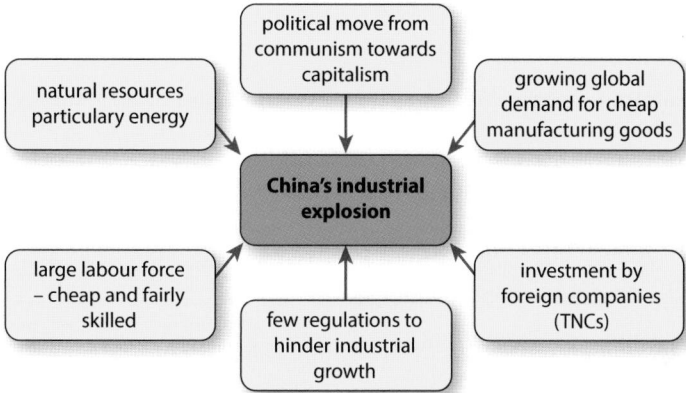

Figure 9.6 *Factors behind China's industrial expansion*

A global development gap?

When the HICs dominated world production and the Soviet Union still existed, it was possible to see the world as divided between a rich north and a poor south. The picture is now more complex than that:

- HICs are still growing richer

- other parts of the world are getting richer too – closing the development gap

- some countries are getting poorer as economic globalisation misses them out.

Stagnating economies

Not all countries have been able to take advantage of economic globalisation. Some are held back by various obstacles: corrupt government, civil war, lack of capital for investment, lack of resources, high levels of international debt.

Global issues (Section D)

Development gaps

As well as varying between countries, development levels also vary within countries:

- some regions experience economic growth while others decline
- often, economic development and wealth are concentrated in the **core** while the **periphery** remains poor.

TOP TIP ✔

Make sure you know a case study of regional disparities within one country, their nature, causes, consequences and management.

Regional development gaps

Core regions often have big advantages, e.g.:

- fertile soils
- close to important markets (trade)
- good communication links
- easy access to energy supplies
- healthy climate, warm climate
- river/sea ports; important trade routes.

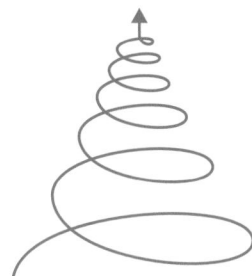

Multiplier effects mean that core regions get richer as development occurs: the core is where the big deals are done.

Periphery regions sometimes have disadvantages:

- poor soils, difficult relief (e.g. mountains)
- they are a long way from the core and its advantages
- communications may be difficult (especially by road)
- lack of energy resources
- diseases may be common (e.g. malaria)
- climate hazards – droughts, floods, etc.

Downwards spiral means that a periphery region gets poorer because anyone who can leave, does leave.

Local development gaps

As well as varying between countries and regions, there are differences between areas, for example within cities – deprivation versus affluence:

- many people in HICs do live in poverty
- some people in LICs live in great wealth.

It is not easy to account for local-scale disparities. These often have long histories and complex causes. Within HIC cities, however, a rich core is often surrounded by a poorer inner city area of run-down, old housing. A suburban zone of middle-income commuters surrounds this.

Rapid population growth

There has been exponential population growth over the last 100 years.

Population growth has been concentrated in LICs. The cause of rapid population growth is a rising birth rate and a falling death rate. This is called **natural increase**.

Consequences for quality of life

Rapid population growth often means huge pressure on resources:

- housing shortages mean a rise in shanty towns and homelessness

- job shortages lead to unemployment, poverty and low living standards

- schools may not have enough places to educate all the children

- infrastructure cannot supply everyone who needs it with power, sanitation, adequate public transport, etc.

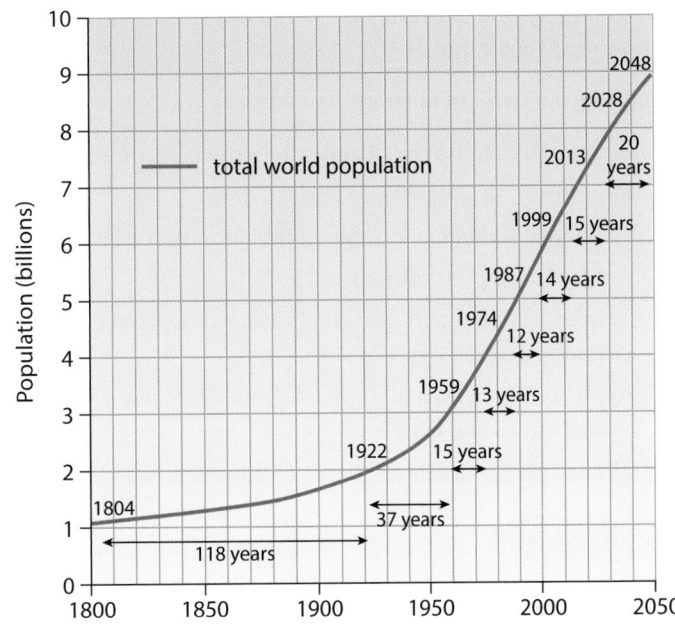

Figure 9.7 *Global population growth, 1800–2050 (projected)*

Medical progress lowers the death rate:
- primary healthcare – preventing disease (e.g. immunisation)
- secondary healthcare – treatment of illnesses

Social, economic and political factors keep the birth rate high:
- not much family planning
- women do not have much education and marry young
- families of five or more children are considered normal
- children work to help support the family
- parents rely on their children in old age
- governments do not provide help with family planning
- religions may not approve of birth control

Figure 9.8 *Factors influencing natural increase in LICs*

Government policies to manage population change

TOP TIP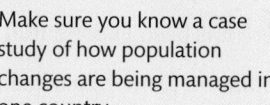

Make sure you know a case study of how population changes are being managed in one country.

Reducing the birth rate

Some birth control programmes work by:

- encouraging and educating people to use birth control methods to limit the size of their families.

Other programmes are different and work by:

- forcing families to use birth control methods through laws.

China's one-child policy is a case study for enforced birth control.

- The one-child policy began in 1979.
- Couples who had only one child received economic rewards and welfare benefits.
- Those couples who had more than one child were fined and did not receive any of the benefits.
- Some women were forced to have very late abortions.

Positive results

- China's population is around 300 million lower than it would have been without the one-child policy, so the policy worked.

Problems and responses

- While the one-child policy worked in the cities, small families are a big problem for traditional farmers.
- Since 2001, couples in rural areas have been allowed to have a second child if the first was a girl.
- Girls are not valued as much as boys. Many girl embryos have been selectively aborted. There are now 120 males for every 100 females.
- The 'Care for Girls' plan in 2004 was a response to this. Girls get free schooling and families with girls have access to better housing and employment.
- Single children will bear the brunt of an aging population: each couple could have four parents and eight grandparents to support.
- There may be a shortage of workers in the future to keep the massive pace of industrialisation in China going.

Another strategy to cope with rapid population growth is Indonesia's transmigration policy. Since the 1960s, millions of people have been moved from overcrowded islands to underpopulated islands.

Increasing the birth rate

Some countries are trying to halt rapidly falling birth rates. Germany is a good example. Couples are encouraged to have more children by tax incentives, long paid maternity and paternity leave, and other benefits.

Managing disparities in development and quality of life

Many different organisations are trying to reduce the development gap between richer areas and poorer areas. Most try to do this by trying to boost development in poorer areas.

TOP TIP
Make sure you know a case study of a UN aid agency project in a LIC.

TOP TIP
Make sure you know a case study of a non-governmental aid agency project in a LIC.

Aid

Most aid comes from governments.

- Multilateral aid is when a government donates aid to an international organisation such as the World Bank. The organisation uses that aid in one of their development projects.

- Bilateral aid is when a government gives aid directly to another government. But this aid usually has strings attached.

Either way, there are problems with aid:

- It is sometimes taken by corrupt governments and never reaches the people it was designed to help.

- It is not always appropriate – for example, sophisticated machinery to pump water for poor rural communities is not appropriate. If it breaks down, who will fix it?

Appropriate aid is aid that is matched to the technology needs and skills of the people who are being helped. It is best if the community involved is able to say what they want and are involved in developing the solutions themselves.

Trade

HICs and Upper MICs have got rich through trade. But once they are rich, they protect their interests with trade blocs and tariffs that make trade unfair for LICs.

- **Fairtrade** agreements set a fair price for products from LICs. They also aim to protect the local environment and help local communities.

- LICs form trade blocs of their own to try to demand fairer trade from HICs and MICs.

Debt relief

High levels of international debt are a major obstacle to development for some stagnating LICs.

- The World Bank's Heavily Indebted Poor Countries Initiative (HIPCI) has cancelled debts for around 30 LICs in return for them investing in social welfare programmes.

1 What development indicator measures the number of births per 1000 people per year? *(1)*

2 What development indicator measures the number of deaths of infants under one year old per year, per 1000 live births in the same year? *(1)*

3 What does HIC stand for? *(1)*

4 A country has a life expectancy at birth of 54.71 years. Is it most likely to be a LIC, MIC or HIC? *(1)*

5 Give **two** reasons why a country's energy consumption would increase as the country develops. *(2)*

6 What is 'quality of life'? *(2)*

7 What does the Human Development Index measure? *(2)*

8 Describe **two** problems with the MIC category of economic development. *(4)*

9 Suggest **two** reasons why one region in a country might be richer than another region. *(4)*

10 Describe **two** consequences that rapid population growth can have on quality of life in LICs. *(4)*

11 **Figure 9.9** shows the North–South divide. Describe the advantages and disadvantages of this model for understanding patterns of development. *(6)*

12 Use a case study to explain the causes and consequences of regional disparities within one country. *(9)*

13 Use a case study to explain how population changes are being managed in one country. *(9)*

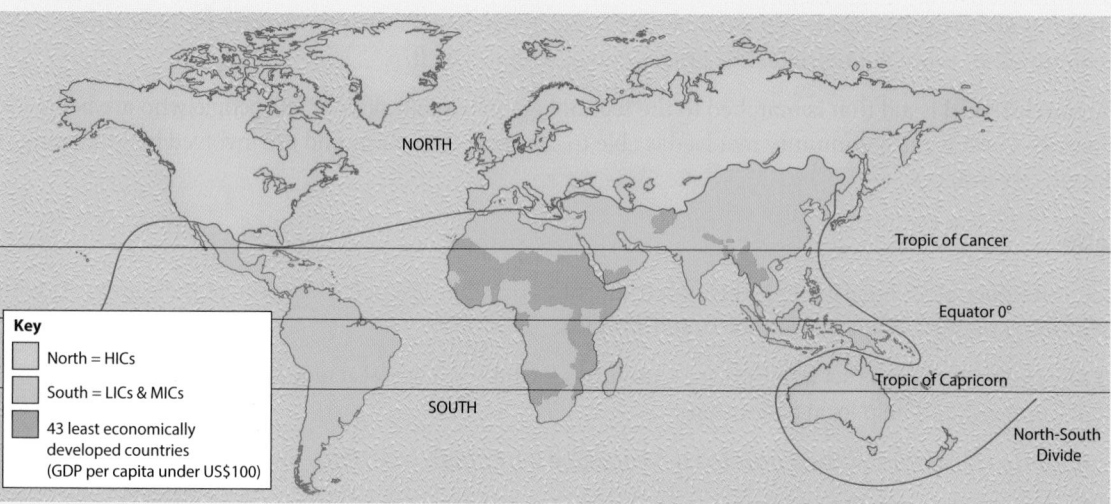

Figure 9.9 *The North–South divide*

Key
- North = HICs
- South = LICs & MICs
- 43 least economically developed countries (GDP per capita under US$100)

NORTH

Tropic of Cancer

Equator 0°

Tropic of Capricorn

SOUTH

North–South Divide

This information applies to the Edexcel International GCSE Geography or Edexcel Certificate Level 1/Level 2 in Geography course. This guide can be used to help revise material from the 2009 specification (with last examination in 2013) and also the 2011 specification (for first examination in 2014). The biggest difference between these specifications is that the practical work has been taken out to form a separate section (Section C) for the 2011 specification, rather than being integrated throughout the units.

About the exam

For your Edexcel International GCSE or Edexcel Certificate Level 1/Level 2 in Geography there is just one external exam which is three hours long.

How many questions do I have to answer?

In this exam you answer **seven** questions in total:

- two questions out of a choice of three in Section A
- two questions out of a choice of three in Section B
- two questions in total in Section C:
  - one question from a choice of two, related to Topics 1 to 3
  - one question from a choice of two, related to Topics 4 to 6
- one question from a choice of three in Section D.

Each question in Sections A, B and C is worth 25 marks.

The Section D question is worth 30 marks.

Section and Topic	Tick the ones you studied
Section A – The natural environment	
Topic 1 – River environments	
Topic 2 – Coastal environments	
Topic 3 – Hazardous environments	
Section B – People and their environments	
Topic 4 – Economic activity and energy	
Topic 5 – Ecosystems and rural environments	
Topic 6 – Urban environments	
Section C – Practical geographical enquiry	
Topic 1 – River environments	
Topic 2 – Coastal environments	
Topic 3 – Hazardous environments	
Topic 4 – Economic activity and energy	
Topic 5 – Ecosystems and rural environments	
Topic 6 – Urban environments	
Section D – Global issues	
Topic 7 – Fragile environments	
Topic 8 – Globalisation and migration	
Topic 9 – Development and human welfare	

TOP TIP

Remember: don't answer more questions than you need to and do answer questions from each section. Use this chart to tick off the topics you studied in each section.

TOP TIP

Make sure you read the exam paper through carefully and calmly. Don't rush and choose a question just because you can answer the first part. Ensure you are choosing the right questions for you – the ones for which you are best prepared.

What sort of questions are in the exam?

Each question is split into different parts:

- In Sections A, B and D each question will be broken down into four parts: a), b), c) and d). Each of those may be broken down further, for example: b) (i), (ii).

- In Section C there are two parts to each question: a) and b). Each part will also be broken down further: (i), (ii), etc.

1–2 mark questions

Each question starts with a stimulus. This could be a photo, a drawing, a map, a graph or a table that is connected to the topic. The first questions will relate directly to this and will test data stimulus skills. These are short questions worth 1 or 2 marks. They might include multiple choice questions, filling in the gap questions or completing tables, for example.

3–4 mark questions

In these questions, as in the 1–2 mark questions, there is 1 mark for each correct point you write. Often these questions will ask you to give a certain number of things, for example 'outline **two** reasons why…' or 'name **three** things that…'. If there are 3 marks available and the question asks you for three things, then each point you write is worth 1 mark. If there are 4 marks available for two things then you need to develop each of the two points a little, for example 'one reason is X, because…' – and add the reason why.

Some 3 or 4 mark questions may ask you to draw or label something (or draw and label), so make sure you practise drawing diagrams as well as revising them.

6 mark questions

These questions often start with the word 'Explain'. This type of question is marked according to levels, so a 6 mark question does not expect you to make six points. Good answers will be clear and detailed and, as you'd expect, be explanatory. Make links between your points so that your explanation is clear and logical. Some 6 mark questions will be about advantages and disadvantages: these questions help, because you have a good framework to hang your answer on.

9 mark questions

These require longer answers than 6 mark questions. They sometimes start with 'Discuss'. You should think of arguments for and arguments against. Some 9 mark questions will ask you to use an example or a case study in your answer. Always make sure you name the example you are using. If the examiner cannot work out what example you are referring to your answer will not be able to get above Level 1 in the mark scheme. If the examiner is clever enough to work out where you are writing about, she or he may be able to mark you in Level 2. But why not make it easy on yourself and write the name of the case study and its location right at the start of your answer?

> **TOP TIP** ✓
> You can use the number of marks available for each part of a question to work out how much time you should allow to answer that part. Allocation of time and effort is critical. You do not want to run out of time on a 6 mark or 9 mark question because you spent too long answering a question that was only worth 2 marks.

> **TOP TIP** ✓
> Make sure you pay close attention to the 'command words' used in the questions, such as 'explain' and 'discuss'. These tell you how the examiner wants you to approach the question.

1 River environments

Store   Places within a system where materials or energy are held for a time

Transfer   Flows of water between stores in the hydrological cycle

Precipitation   The deposition of moisture on the Earth's surface, in the form of dew, frost, rain, hail, sleet, snow

Watershed   The dividing line between one drainage basin and another

Channel network   The system of tributary streams that join increasingly large river channels in a drainage basin

River regime   The seasonal pattern of river discharge over the course of a year

Discharge   The quantity of water that passes a given point on a river bank within a set period of time

Hydrograph   A graph showing a river's rate of discharge over time as it goes past a specific point

Erosion   The wearing down of land by water, ice, wind and gravity

Weathering   The chemical alteration and physical breakdown of rock in its original position

Mass movement   The movement of weathered rock down slope without the direct action of running water

Meander   A pronounced bend in a river

Water quality   A measure of how fit water is for human consumption. Polluted water has low water quality

2 Coastal environments

Sub-aerial processes   The general re-shaping of the land by normal atmospheric processes, for example wind and rain; includes weathering, mass movement, erosion and deposition

Longshore drift   The movement of loose materials along a coastline by wave action because waves break at an oblique angle to the shore

Ecosystem   An organic community of plants and animals interacting with their environment

Coral reef   A marine ecosystem formed by reef-building corals

Mangroves   Tropical and sub-tropical coastal forests; mangrove trees can grow in salty, tidal water

Sand dunes   Coastal sand hills above the high tide mark covered with grasses and shrubs

Salt marsh   A tidal ecosystem in estuaries and deltas consisting of mud flats with salt-tolerant grasses and plants

Biodiversity   The variety of species in an ecosystem

Hard engineering   The use of concrete and large artificial structures by civil engineers to defend land against natural erosion processes

Soft engineering   Managing erosion by working with natural processes to help restore beaches and coastal ecosystems

3 Hazardous environments

Hazard   A natural event that threatens or causes damage, destruction or death

Disaster (natural)   The results of a natural hazard taking place, such as deaths, injuries and destruction of property

Earthquake   A sudden or violent movement within the Earth's crust followed by a series of shocks

Volcano   An opening in the Earth's crust out of which lava, ash and gases erupt

Tropical storms   An area of low pressure with winds moving in a spiral around the central point, called the eye of the storm. Winds are powerful and there is heavy rainfall

Monitoring   Recording physical changes, such as earthquake tremors around a volcano or tracking a tropical storm by satellite, to help predict when and where a natural hazard might strike

Prediction   Being able to say when and where a natural hazard will strike

Mitigation   Reducing the risk from natural hazards before they happen, such as building earthquake-proof buildings

Aid   Help given by more wealthy nations to less well-off nations, mainly to encourage development or recover from a natural disaster

Disaster relief   Immediate help given after a disaster, including emergency responses such as sending firefighters and search and rescue teams

4   Economic activity and energy

LIC   Low Income Country

MIC   Middle Income Country

HIC   High Income Country

Sectoral shift   The gradual change from an economy based on primary sectors to one based on secondary, tertiary and then quaternary sectors

Informal sector   This is largely made up of jobs over which there is little or no official control

Location   The site/place where a shop, factory or office is found. Businesses think carefully about where to locate, taking into account many factors

Accessibility   The ease with which people can get to a particular place

Hi-tech industry   Manufacturing involving advanced technology, including ICT, genetic engineering

TNC   Transnational corporation – a large enterprise that operates on a global scale and is involved in a wide variety of businesses

Development   The way a country progresses and improves over time, usually measured by rising incomes and better quality of life

Energy gap   The difference between the demand for energy and the supply of it

Non-renewable   A material that cannot be restored after use. Examples include fossil fuels and minerals

Renewable   A resource that is not diminished when it is used; it cannot be exhausted (e.g. wind and tidal energy)

5   Ecosystems and rural environments

Biome   A world-scale ecosystem usually defined by the dominant vegetation, for example the tropical rainforest

Adaptation   The way plants and animals have evolved to cope with the conditions they live in

Succession   The change over time in the plants that colonize an area until the final ecosystem, such as temperate grassland, is developed

Temperate grassland   A biome found in the mid-latitude interiors of continents dominated by grasses and rich soils

Food web   In an ecosystem, a food web shows what is eating what, and therefore how energy moves from plants to animals

Rural   The countryside, non-urbanised areas. Many rural areas have small settlements, low population densities and open space used for farming

GM   Crops and livestock that have been genetically modified to improve productivity and disease resistance

Irrigation   The supply of water to the land by means of channels, streams and sprinklers in order to permit the growing of crops in dry areas

HYVs   High Yielding Varieties of cereal crops developed to increase yields

Rural–urban migration   People moving from the countryside to live in towns and cities

Depopulation (rural)   People leaving the countryside, often to go to urban areas, so rural population declines

Counterurbanisation   The movement of people and activities away from large cities to small towns, villages or the countryside

6   Urban environments

Urbanisation   The process of becoming more urban, mainly through more and more people living in towns and cities

Suburbanisation   The spread of low density, often detached or semi-detached housing around the edges of a city or town

Megacity   A city with a population over 10 million

Inner city   City area, close to the CBD, characterized by old housing, poor services and brownfield sites

Self help (housing)   When people in shanty towns gradually improve their own housing and surroundings. Often they are helped by a NGO

Rural – urban fringe   An area on the outskirts of a city where land use is contested between rural and urban uses

Brownfield site   Land that has been used, abandoned and now awaits a new use. Commonly found in urban areas, particularly in the inner city

Greenfield site   A plot of land, often in a rural area or on the edge of an urban area, that has not yet been built on or developed

Deprivation   When people lack what the rest of society considers 'normal', such as good housing, reasonable incomes or access to healthcare

Urban regeneration   The revival of old parts of the built-up area by either installing modern facilities in old buildings (known as renewal) or opting for redevelopment

Rebranding   Urban regeneration that also tries to give an area a new image. Rebranded areas often have names and logos, e.g. MediaCityUK in Salford

7   Fragile environments

Sustainability   Actions that meet the needs of the present without reducing the ability of future generations to meet their needs

Soil erosion   The removal of soil by wind and water and by the movement of soil down slope

Desertification   The spread of desert-like conditions into semi-arid areas

Deforestation   The felling and clearance of forested land by humans

Malnutrition   When people lack a balanced, sufficient diet

Famine   A widespread, serious shortage of food. In the worst cases it can lead to starvation and deaths

Migration   When people move from one area to another

Global warming   A slow but significant rise in the Earth's temperature

Enhanced greenhouse effect   The warming of the Earth's atmosphere because pollution is preventing heat from escaping into space

8   Globalisation and migration

Globalisation   The process that has created a more connected world, with increases in the movements of goods (trade) and people (migration and tourism) worldwide

Production chains   The stages by which businesses obtain and process commodities and transform them into manufactured goods

Mass tourism   Holidays where travel and accommodation are put together by a tour operator; these are often relatively cheap holidays to popular places

Ecotourism   A type of tourism that aims to conserve fragile ecosystems and ensure that its benefits (jobs, income) stay within the local area

Net migration   The balance between the number of immigrants (people entering) and emigrants (people leaving) a country

Voluntary migration   The movement of people who have chosen to move rather than being forced to move

Forced migration   The movement of people caused by a push factor such as famine, war or religious persecution

Asylum seekers   Forced migrants who have asked for permission to permanently reside in the country they have migrated to

Refugees   People who flee their country to avoid war, the threat of death, oppression or persecution

9   Development and human welfare

GDP   Gross domestic product – the total value of goods and services produced by a country during a year

GNI   Gross national income – very similar to GDP but also takes into account that some countries are in debt and pay money in interest on their debt

Quality of life   A social measure, an umbrella term that takes into account both GDP and human welfare

HDI   Human development index. Used as a measure of development in a country and for making international comparisons

Literacy   The ability to read and write

Life expectancy   The average number of years a person might be expected to live

Emerging economies   Countries that are developing and industrialising rapidly

Development gap   The difference between countries with the lowest development indicators and those with the highest

Core   The most economically and politically dominant area in a country or region

Periphery   The more isolated, less economically developed and less politically influential area in a country or region

Appropriate aid   Know-how and equipment that are suited to the basic conditions prevailing in the country receiving the aid

Index

ndex

eadings in **bold** are glossary terms.